OHIO
COOK BOOK

Cooking Across America
Cookbook Collection™

**GOLDEN
WEST ☼
PUBLISHERS**

Front cover photo courtesy Ohio Pork Producers Council, Westerville

Compiled by Donna Goodrich

Recipes on pages 28, 34 & 45 courtesy of:
Ohio Sea Grant Publications
Ohio State University
1314 Kinnear Road, Columbus, OH 43212-1194.

Recipes on pages 38 & 48 courtesy of:
Junior League of Cincinnati
"I'll cook when pigs fly . . . and they do in Cincinnati"
3500 Columbia Parkway, Cincinnati, OH 45226-2109
(513) 871-9339.

ISBN – 1-885590-47-4

Printed in the United States of America

Golden West Publishers, Inc.
4113 N. Longview Ave.
Phoenix, AZ 85014, USA
(602) 265-4392

Visit our website: http://www.goldenwestpublishers.com

★ ★ ★ ★ *Ohio Cook Book* ★ ★ ★ ★

Table of Contents

★ ★ ★ ★ *Cooking Across America* ★ ★ ★ ★

Table of Contents (continued)

Introduction

Ohio is a land of breathtaking splendor, pastoral beauty and urban vitality. While small towns and family farms fill the Buckeye State, its towns and cities teem with a blend of established businesses and new growth and development. Ohio is the birthplace of inventors, the mother of presidents and home to generations of free thinkers and hard workers. Today's Ohio is a testament to the "can do" attitude of its inhabitants.

The *Ohio Cook Book* is filled with wonderful and delicious recipes that represent the best of Ohio's great culinary heritage. Fresh produce, meats and seafood are featured in a tantalizing array of mouth-watering family favorites. From Bed and Breakfasts, family farms, restaurants and food manufacturers, these recipes represent a wide variety of ethnic flavors.

From Lake Erie to the Ohio River and Cincinnati to Youngstown, *Ohio Cook Book* presents a rich introduction to the people and lifestyles that make up this great state. As part of the *Cooking Across America Cookbook Collection* this book provides you with a delicious taste of Ohio!

★ ★ ★ ★ *Cooking Across America* ★ ★ ★ ★

Ohio Facts

Size—35th largest state with an area of 40,953 square miles
Population—11,353,140
State Capital—Columbus
Statehood—March 1, 1803, the 17th state
    admitted to the Union
State Name: From Iroquois Indian word
    for "great/good river"
State Nickname—Buckeye State
State Song—"Beautiful Ohio" words by
    Ballard MacDonald, music by Mary Earl
    (with special lyrics by Wilbert. B. McBride)
State Motto—*"With God, all things are possible."*
State Bird—Cardinal
State Beverage—Tomato Juice

State Tree
Ohio Buckeye

State Flower
Scarlet Carnation

Famous Ohioans

Neil Armstrong, *astronaut;* **George Bellows,** *painter/lithographer;* **Willard H. Bennett,** *inventor;* **Ambrose Bierce,** *journalist;* **Erma Bombeck,** *columnist/humorist;* **Bill Boyd** (Hopalong Cassidy), *actor;* **William Jennings Bryan,** *U.S. presidential candidate;* **George Custer,** *army officer;* **Dorothy Dandridge,** *actress;* **Doris Day,** *singer/actress;* **Clarence Darrow,** *lawyer;* **Ruby Dee,** *actress;* **Hugh Downs,** TV broadcaster; **Thomas Edison,** *inventor;* **Clark Gable,** *actor;* **Lillian Gish,** *actress;* **John Glenn,** *astronaut/senator;* **Zane Grey,** *author;* **Dean Martin,** *singer/actor;* **Paul Newman,** *actor;* **Jack Nicklaus,** *golfer;* **Annie Oakley,** *markswoman;* **Norman Vincent Peale,** *clergyman;* **Tyrone Power,** *actor;* **Judith Resnik,** *astronaut;* **Eddie Rickenbacker,** *aviator;* **Arthur M. Schlesinger, Jr.,** *historian;* **William T. Sherman,** *army general;* **Steven Spielberg,** *director/screenwriter;* **Gloria Steinem,** *feminist;* **Tecumseh,** *Shawnee Indian chief;* **Ted Turner,** *broadcasting;* **Lowell Thomas,** *commentator/author;* **James Thurber,** *author/cartoonist;* **Orville Wright,** *inventor;* **Cy Young,** *baseball player.*

Ohio Presidents

Ulysses S. Grant Rutherford B. Hayes James Garfield Benjamin Harrison William McKinley William H. Taft Warren G. Harding
(18th)   (19th)   (20th)   (23rd)   (25th)   (27th)   (29th)

For Information: Ohio Division of Travel & Tourism: 614-466-8844

Appetizers & Beverages

Poor Nick's Caviar

"My husband gave me this recipe when we were married over 58 years ago. He made this for me on our first anniversary, as we could not afford real caviar. This is an appetizer called 'Ikra' that he ate in Russia when he was a boy."

Norma K. Czaruk—Wintersville

1 EGGPLANT
3 Tbsp. OLIVE OIL
1 ONION, diced
1 TOMATO, diced
1 clove GARLIC, minced
2 Tbsp. LEMON JUICE
SUGAR
SALT and PEPPER
Chopped fresh PARSLEY

Pierce eggplant, place in a baking dish and bake at 350° until tender; allow to cool. Peel eggplant and finely chop. In a skillet, heat oil and sauté onion until translucent. Add tomato and eggplant and sauté for 3-5 minutes; stir in garlic and lemon juice. Season with sugar and salt and pepper to taste; add parsley as desired. Serve warm or chilled with party rye bread or crackers.

Barbecued Meatballs

"A co-worker gave me this recipe for the wonderful meatballs she serves at her Christmas parties. Everyone loves them!"

Pamela S. Furlong—Greenville

Meatballs:

3 lbs. GROUND BEEF	1-2 cups QUICK OATS
1 can (12 oz.) EVAPORATED MILK	2 tsp. CHILI POWDER
1 1/2 tsp. GARLIC POWDER	2 EGGS, lightly beaten

Sauce:

2 cups KETCHUP	1 tsp. LIQUID SMOKE
1 1/2 cups packed BROWN SUGAR	1 tsp. GARLIC POWDER

In a bowl, combine meatball ingredients and mix well. Form into 1-inch balls and place in a large roasting pan or two 13 x 9 baking pans. In a bowl, combine all sauce ingredients; mix well. Pour sauce evenly over meatballs, cover with foil and bake at 375° for 45-50 minutes.

Sausage Swirls

"These are great to serve as appetizers."

Donna Marie Schlabach—Donna's Premier Lodging, Berlin

4 cups FLOUR	1 tsp. SALT
1/4 cup CORNMEAL	2/3 cup VEGETABLE OIL
2 Tbsp. SUGAR	3/4 cup MILK
2 tsp. BAKING POWDER	2 lbs. BULK PORK SAUSAGE

In a bowl, combine flour, cornmeal, sugar, baking powder and salt. Stir in oil until mixture resembles coarse crumbs. Gradually stir in enough milk to form a soft dough. Turn dough out onto a floured surface; knead lightly for 30 seconds. Roll dough into two (16 x 10) rectangles. Crumble sausage over dough to within 1/2-inch on all sides. Carefully roll up from the 16-inch end. Wrap in foil and chill for at least 1 hour. Cut into 1/2-inch slices and place one inch apart on ungreased baking sheets. Bake at 400° for 15-20 minutes or until lightly browned. Serve warm or cold; store in refrigerator.

Makes 4 dozen.

Hall of Fame Queso Dip

"For pre-parade parties during our Pro Football Hall of Fame activities, this dip will be a hit! Canton is also known as the birthplace of the National Football League."

Theresa Stotler—Canton

2 cans (10.75 oz. ea.) CHEDDAR CHEESE SOUP
1/2 cup WATER
1/4 lb. PEPPERONI, diced
1 jar (16 oz.) MEDIUM-HOT PICANTE SALSA
8 slices VELVEETA®
1/3 cup shredded MOZZARELLA CHEESE
1/3 cup shredded CHEDDAR or SHARP CHEDDAR CHEESE

In a large saucepan, combine soup and water and mix well. Cook on medium heat until soup begins to bubble. Add pepperoni, salsa and Velveeta; stir until Velveeta is melted. Just before serving, toss in mozzarella and cheddar cheeses and stir. Serve with chips.

Reuben Roll-ups

"Waynesville is well-known for its sauerkraut festivals."

Connie Combs—Beavercreek

1 pkg. (8 oz.) refrigerator CRESCENT ROLLS
8 thin slices cooked CORNED BEEF
1 can (8 oz.) SAUERKRAUT, drained
1 Tbsp. THOUSAND ISLAND DRESSING
2 slices SWISS CHEESE, cut in 1/2-inch strips

Preheat oven to 350°. Unroll crescent rolls and separate into triangles. Place sliced corned beef across wide end of each triangle. Combine sauerkraut with salad dressing; spread 2 tablespoons of mixture on corned beef. Top with 2 strips of cheese. Roll up, beginning at wide end of triangle and place on an ungreased baking sheet. Bake for 10-15 minutes or until golden brown. Remove from oven and slice each into thirds. Serve warm.

Microwave Swedish Meatballs

"You'll want to double the recipe the next time you make this–they are delicious!"

Shelley Szermeta—Fremont

1 lb. GROUND CHUCK	1/2 tsp. SALT
1 EGG, lightly beaten	1/8 tsp. ALLSPICE
1/2 cup dry BREAD CRUMBS	1/8 tsp. PEPPER
1/2 cup MILK, divided	1 can (10.75 oz.) CREAM
1/4 cup finely diced ONION	OF MUSHROOM SOUP
2 tsp. PARSLEY FLAKES	

In a mixing bowl, combine ground chuck, egg, bread crumbs, 1/4 cup milk, onion, parsley and seasonings; mix well. Shape mixture into 1 1/4-inch balls and arrange in a baking dish. Cook for 8-9 minutes on Medium-High, turning once halfway through cooking time. In a bowl, blend soup with remaining milk until smooth. Pour over meatballs. Cover and cook for an additional 4-6 minutes.

Artichoke Spread

"A dear friend shared this recipe with me years ago and it is a big hit everywhere I take it."

Saundra Preston—Springboro

1 can (14 oz.) ARTICHOKE HEARTS,
    drained and cut into small pieces
1 cup grated PARMESAN CHEESE
1 cup MAYONNAISE
CRACKERS or CHIPS

Preheat oven to 350°. In a bowl, combine artichoke hearts, Parmesan cheese and mayonnaise and stir well. Spread mixture in a glass pie pan or shallow casserole dish that has been sprayed with cooking spray. Bake for 20-25 minutes or until top is golden brown. Serve with crackers or chips.

Donna's Nachos

"This recipe came from a niece who is an excellent cook! It's a favorite at all of our family gatherings."

Joan Konkle—Spencerville

1 can (9 oz.) JALAPEÑO
  BEAN DIP
2-3 AVOCADOS, mashed
1 Tbsp. LEMON JUICE
SALT and PEPPER
1 cup SOUR CREAM
1/2 cup MAYONNAISE

TACO SEASONING MIX, to taste
1 bunch GREEN ONIONS, diced
2 cups chopped RIPE OLIVES
3 cups grated CHEDDAR
  CHEESE
3 TOMATOES, diced
TORTILLA CHIPS

On a serving platter, spread bean dip in a large circle. In a bowl, combine avocados, lemon juice, salt and pepper to taste and mix well. Spread over bean dip. Combine sour cream, mayonnaise and taco seasoning and mix well. Spread over avocado mixture. Layer onions, olives, cheese and tomatoes over sour cream mixture. Refrigerate several hours before serving. Serve with tortilla chips.

Did You Know?
The Ohio State flag is the only pennant-shaped state flag in the United States!

Swiss Cheese Canapés

Carol Sebald—Guggisberg Cheese Factory, Millersberg

2 pkgs. (6.5 oz. ea.) REFRIGERATED BUTTERMILK BISCUITS
3 cups shredded GUGGISBERG® SWISS CHEESE
2 cups MAYONNAISE
1 Tbsp. grated ONION
PAPRIKA

Bake biscuits as per package directions. Cool and then split in half. Place halves face up on cookie sheet. In a bowl, combine cheese, mayonnaise and onion. Spread on tops of biscuits and sprinkle with paprika. Bake at 350° for 5-10 minutes or until cheese bubbles.

Chalet in the Valley Cheese Fondue

Chef Jeff—Chalet Kitchen–Guggisberg Cheese Factory,
Millersberg

**12 oz. shredded GUGGISBERG®
BABY SWISS CHEESE
4 oz. shredded GRUYÈRE CHEESE
1 Tbsp. CORNSTARCH
1/2 clove GARLIC, minced
6 oz. SAUTERNE WINE
2 Tbsp. DRY SHERRY**

Combine both cheeses and cornstarch and freeze for at least one day. Thaw in refrigerator or microwave. In a medium saucepan, sauté garlic then add sauterne. Bring to a boil, whisk in thawed cheese mixture, stirring constantly, until smoooth and bubbly. Stir in sherry, reduce heat to a simmer. Place mixture in a fondue pot over medium to low heat. Dip French bread cubes, bread or vegetable sticks.

Pawpaw Lassi

"This recipe, (created by Casa Nueva Restaurant in Athens, Ohio), won first place in the drinks category of our 1999 Pawpaw Festival Cook-off."

Chris Chmiel—Integration Acres/Ohio Pawpaw Growers
Association, Albany

**1/2 cup WATER
4 cups YOGURT
2/3 cup HONEY**

**1/2 tsp. SALT
1 cup PAWPAW PULP
1/2 tsp. CINNAMON**

Blend all ingredients together thoroughly, pour into tall glasses and serve.

About Pawpaws

The pawpaw tree, native to North America, bears a small green and yellow fruit that looks somewhat like a thick, short banana. The yellow pulp of the fruit has a sweet flavor reminiscent of bananas, pears and pineapple.

Breakfast & Brunch

Cinnamon Logs

"This is a favorite at our Bed & Breakfast. Served before breakfast, on the front porch with coffee, it's delicious!"
Linda Rockaway—Rockaway Bed & Breakfast, Kelleys Island

1 loaf (16 oz.) thinly sliced WHITE BREAD, crusts trimmed
1 pkg. (8 oz.) CREAM CHEESE, softened
1 EGG WHITE
1/2 cup POWDERED SUGAR
1 cup SUGAR
1 Tbsp. CINNAMON
1/2 cup BUTTER, melted

Roll bread slices out to 1/4-inch thickness. In a bowl, beat cream cheese, egg white and powdered sugar at medium speed with electric mixer until smooth. Spread mixture evenly on one side of each bread slice; roll up to form "logs." Stir together sugar and cinnamon in a shallow dish. Brush logs with butter, then roll in sugar mixture. Place logs on a wire rack placed over baking sheet. Bake at 350° for 15 minutes. Remove from oven and cool before serving.

Makes 1 1/2 dozen.

Blueberry Stuffed French Toast

"My sister gave us this recipe as soon as we received approval to open our Bed & Breakfast. It was a favorite of hers and has proven to be a big hit! My husband's parents pick fresh blueberries for us each summer to use in this recipe."

Debra & Tom Fitzgerald—Fitzgerald's Irish Bed & Breakfast, Painesville

6 EGGS	1 cup fresh or frozen
1 tsp. grated ORANGE PEEL	BLUEBERRIES, thawed
2/3 cup ORANGE JUICE	8 slices (1 1/4-inch thick)
3 Tbsp. SUGAR, divided	ITALIAN BREAD
Pinch of SALT	1/3 cup sliced ALMONDS

Preheat oven to 400°. In a bowl, beat eggs, orange peel, orange juice, 2 tablespoons sugar and salt until well blended. Pour into a 13 x 9 baking pan that has been sprayed with cooking spray and set aside. In a small bowl, combine blueberries with remaining sugar and set aside. With the tip of a knife, cut a 1-1 1/2-inch "pocket" in the side of each bread slice. Fill pockets with blueberry mixture. Place filled slices in egg mixture; let stand, turning once, until egg mixture is absorbed (about 15 minutes). Sprinkle with almonds. Bake for 10 minutes, turn slices over and continue to bake for 5 minutes. Serve with ***Blueberry-Orange Sauce.***

Blueberry-Orange Sauce

3 Tbsp. SUGAR	1 cup fresh or frozen
1 Tbsp. CORNSTARCH	BLUEBERRIES
1/8 tsp. SALT	2 ORANGES,
1/4 cup ORANGE JUICE	peeled and sectioned
1/4 cup WATER	

In a bowl, combine sugar, cornstarch and salt and set aside. In a small saucepan, combine orange juice and water; bring to a boil. Add blueberries and orange sections. Bring to a boil again and cook for 2 minutes. Stir in sugar mixture and continue to cook until sauce thickens.

Too Easy To Be True Oatmeal

"We truly enjoy serving this to our guests at our Bed & Breakfast. This is wonderful on cold mornings in Ohio."
Maryann & Hank Burwinkel—The Empty Nest Bed & Breakfast,
Cincinnati

2 cups MILK
1 cup QUICK OATS
1 tsp. BUTTER
1 EGG, beaten

SUGAR or BROWN SUGAR
CINNAMON
NUTMEG

Combine milk, oats, butter and egg in a crockpot, adding sugar, cinnamon and nutmeg to taste. Set heat on Low and start cooking the night before planning to serve. Cook 6-8 hours.

Summer House Strata

"This recipe is absolutely delicious!"
Jo Lane Elson—Elson Inn Bed & Breakfast, Magnolia

1 loaf "day old" ITALIAN BREAD
2/3 cup chopped HAM
2/3 cup chopped SWISS CHEESE
  or CHEDDAR CHEESE

3 EGGS
2 1/2 cups MILK
2 Tbsp. MUSTARD
3 Tbsp. OLIVE OIL

Cut Italian bread into 1/2-inch cubes. Spray a 10-inch quiche or pie pan with cooking spray. Generously fill pan with bread cubes, adding extra in the center. Sprinkle ham and cheese on top of bread. In a bowl, combine remaining ingredients and beat well. Pour over all, cover with plastic wrap and refrigerate overnight. Remove pan from refrigerator 45 minutes before baking. Preheat oven to 375°. Bake for 15 minutes or until set and top is golden. If top browns too quickly, cover loosely with foil until strata is done.

Serves 6-8.

Note: Strata tends to deflate when removed from oven.

Italian Sausage Breakfast Pie

"This is my great-grandmother's recipe and a favorite for Easter or on Sundays after church. It is also a great dish to take to picnics."

Gloria Cipri Kemer—Emerald Necklace Inn Bed & Breakfast,
Fairview Park-Cleveland

Prepare a **BISCUIT DOUGH** adding **1 Tbsp. SUGAR** to mixture. Make enough dough to form a lining, 1/4-inch thick, in a 12 x 12 x 2 baking dish plus enough dough to make 8 (1/2-inch wide) strips, for a lattice-style top crust. Coat baking dish with **MARGARINE** and dust with **FLOUR**. Line dish with dough, forming to bottom and sides; let stand for 30 minutes to dry before adding *Italian Sausage Filling*. Top with alternating dough strips to create lattice pattern. In a small bowl, beat reserved egg white from filling with **1 Tbsp. WATER** until frothy, then brush on dough strips. Bake at 350° for 1 hour or until top has lightly browned. Allow to cool before cutting.

Italian Sausage Filling

1-1 1/2 lbs. ITALIAN SAUSAGE	1/2 tsp. ONION SALT
7 EGGS, 1 white reserved	1/2 tsp. ONION POWDER
1 cup grated ROMANO CHEESE	1/2 tsp. PEPPER
	Pinch of SALT
1 cup RICOTTA CHEESE	1/4 cup PARSLEY

In a skillet; brown sausage; drain and cool to room temperature. In a large mixing bowl, beat eggs. Add sausage and remaining ingredients and mix well.

Bob Evans, Down at the Farm

In 1948, Bob Evans made sausages for his 12-stool restaurant in nearby Gallipolis. Today, Bob Evans Farms Inc. owns and operates more than 460 full-service restaurants in a 22-state area. Each year, in mid-October, the 1,000-acre Bob Evans Farm in Rio Grande is host to a gala festival that celebrates the history and culture of the region.

Hawaiian French Toast

"Our guests have enjoyed this signature recipe at our Bed & Breakfast since 1987! My predecessor, Toni Kohlstedt, passed it along to me when I acquired the Inn."

Marge Pendleton—The Duck Pond Bed & Breakfast, Oxford

4 EGGS	1/4 lb. BUTTER
1/3 cup MILK	(no substitutes)
2/3 cup ORANGE JUICE	Ground MACADAMIA
1/4 cup SUGAR	NUTS
1/4 tsp. NUTMEG	
1/2 tsp. VANILLA	Coconut glaze:
8 slices (1-inch thick) FRENCH	CREAM of COCONUT
BREAD	LIGHT KARO® SYRUP

In a bowl, whisk together eggs, milk, orange juice, sugar, nutmeg and vanilla. Place bread in a cake pan that has a tight fitting lid. Pour egg mixture over bread; turn slices over to coat both sides. Cover and refrigerate overnight. Melt butter on a large cookie sheet. Dip each slice of soaked bread in butter, turn over and sprinkle with nuts to taste. Bake at 350° for 25-30 minutes or until golden brown. To prepare coconut glaze: In a small saucepan, mix equal parts of cream of coconut and Karo syrup; warm and pour over French toast.

Serves 4.

Columbus

Columbus has pioneered in several areas of education. In 1837, the city began the nation's first state school for the blind and in 1909 the first junior high school in the U.S. opened. In 1922, Ohio State University founded WOSU, the first educational radio station in North America. Today, visitors can enjoy the shops and restaurants of German Village, a restored German settlement of the 1800's or Ohio Village, a reconstruction of a 19th-century rural Ohio community. In August, Columbus is home to the Ohio State Fair, one of the largest fairs in the nation!

Egg & Cheese Filled Crepes with Dill Sauce

"This crepe recipe is from my Hungarian mother-in-law. The sauce is mine, using fresh dill from my herb garden."

Sue Tarr—Ivy & Lace Bed & Breakfast, Hartville

Crepes:

2 EGGS	2 tsp. SUGAR
Pinch of SALT	1 1/2 tsp. VANILLA
1 cup FLOUR	1 1/2 Tbsp. BUTTER,
1 1/2 cups MILK	melted

Filling:
1 1/2 lg. EGGS per crepe
MUENSTER CHEESE, cut into small pieces

Fresh DILL sprigs

Crepe preparation: In a blender, combine all crepe ingredients, except butter. Blend on low speed for 1 minute. Scrape down sides, add butter and blend for 15 seconds. Refrigerate for 1 hour; stir before cooking. In a crepe pan or small skillet, heat a small amount of oil. Pour in 1/4 cup crepe batter; quickly tilt pan to allow batter to form a thin, even coating over bottom. Let cook for 1-2 minutes or until crepe just begins to brown. Turn and brown the other side. Continue until all batter is used, placing waxed paper between each crepe as it is made*. Scramble eggs in a skillet and cook until done. Place eggs down the middle of each crepe, sprinkle with muenster cheese to taste and fold over sides. Spoon *Dill Sauce* on top and garnish with a sprig of fresh dill.

*Crepes can be wrapped in foil or plastic and refrigerated 2-3 days. If refrigerated, reheat for 30 seconds in microwave.

Dill Sauce

2 Tbsp. BUTTER, melted	1 cup MILK
1 Tbsp. FLOUR	Fresh chopped DILL
Pinch of SALT	

In a saucepan, combine all ingredients and cook over medium heat until thickened. Add more milk if needed.

Country Sausage Gravy

"This gravy can be served over biscuits or potatoes. It has a hearty flavor and is easy to prepare."

Donna Marie Schlabach—Donna's Premier Lodging, Berlin

1 lb. SAUSAGE
1 can (10.75 oz.) CREAM OF CHICKEN SOUP
1 can MILK
1/2 tsp. DRY MUSTARD
1/4 tsp. SEASONED SALT
1/4 tsp. PEPPER
1 cup SOUR CREAM

In a heavy skillet, crumble sausage and cook over medium heat until browned; drain and set aside. In the same skillet, blend soup and milk together. Add mustard, salt and pepper and bring to a boil. Reduce heat and stir in sausage and sour cream. Simmer until heated through but do not boil.

Serves 4-6.

Apple French Toast

"This is a very popular breakfast for our guests. It features apples, one of Ohio's largest crops."

Nancy Purdy—Bailey House Bed & Breakfast, Georgetown

1 stick BUTTER
1 cup packed BROWN SUGAR
2 Tbsp. LIGHT KARO® SYRUP
4 lg. APPLES, peeled and sliced
3 EGGS

1 cup MILK
1 Tbsp. VANILLA
8 slices (3/4-inch thick)
    FRENCH BREAD

In a saucepan, melt butter; add brown sugar and syrup. Cook over medium heat until bubbly. Pour mixture into a greased 13 x 9 pan. Layer apples on top. In a bowl, beat eggs; add milk and vanilla and mix well. Dip bread into egg mixture and layer over top of apples. Cover and refrigerate overnight. Bake, uncovered, at 350° for 35 minutes. To serve, invert each slice of bread onto serving plates; spoon apples over top.

Serves 4.

Apple Crumb Coffee Cake

"This winning recipe was submitted by the Ohio Fruit and Vegetable Growers Association in Columbus and was published in the Ohio Apple Marketing Program recipe book."

Royetta Floriana—Fremont

1 box (18.25 oz.) YELLOW CAKE MIX
3/4 cup VEGETABLE OIL
1/4 cup SUGAR
4 EGGS
1 ctn. (8 oz.) LOW FAT SOUR CREAM
2 cups chopped JONATHAN APPLES
1 cup packed BROWN SUGAR
1 tsp. CINNAMON
1 cup chopped PECANS or WALNUTS

Glaze:

2 cups POWDERED SUGAR	1 tsp. VANILLA
4 Tbsp. MILK	2 Tbsp. BUTTER, melted

Preheat oven to 350°. In a mixing bowl, combine cake mix, oil, sugar, eggs and sour cream and mix well. Fold in apples. Pour 1/2 of cake mixture into a 13 x 9 cake pan that has been sprayed with cooking spray. In another bowl, combine brown sugar, cinnamon and nuts; sprinkle 1/2 of mixture over cake. Swirl sugar-nut mixture throughout the cake with a small knife. Pour remaining cake batter into pan and sprinkle with remaining sugar-nut mixture. Swirl the topping lightly into the top layer. Bake for 50-60 minutes. To prepare glaze: In a small bowl, combine all ingredients and mix well. When cake is removed from oven, pierce holes in top with toothpicks or tines of a fork. Pour glaze over cake while still warm; allow to cool for 1 hour before serving.

The J. M. Smucker Company

Jerome Monroe Smucker first pressed cider, from apples that grew on trees Johnny Appleseed had planted, at a mill he opened in Orrville in 1897. Today the worldwide J. M. Smucker company is still headquartered in Orrville!

Blueberry French Toast

"This is an unusual recipe that makes a great first impression when served. I have served this delicious breakfast quite often since opening our Bed & Breakfast; everyone requests the recipe."

Rose & Roger Riepenhoff—Rose Haven Bed & Breakfast, Ottawa

12 slices DAY-OLD WHITE BREAD, cut into 1-inch cubes
2 pkgs. (8 oz. ea.) CREAM CHEESE, cut into 1-inch cubes
1 cup fresh or frozen BLUEBERRIES
12 EGGS
2 cups HALF AND HALF
1/3 cup MAPLE SYRUP or HONEY

Place 1/2 of bread cubes in a greased 13 x 9 baking dish. Layer with cream cheese. Top with blueberries and remaining bread cubes. In a bowl, beat eggs; add half and half and syrup and mix well. Pour mixture over bread. Cover and refrigerate 8 hours or overnight. Remove from refrigerator 30 minutes before baking. Bake, covered, at 350° for 30 minutes; uncover and bake for an additional 25-30 minutes or until top is golden brown and center is set. Serve with warm *Blueberry Sauce* on top.

Blueberry Sauce

1 cup SUGAR
2 Tbsp. CORNSTARCH
1 cup WATER

1 cup fresh or frozen BLUEBERRIES
1 Tbsp. BUTTER

In a saucepan, combine sugar and cornstarch, then add water. Bring to a boil over medium heat and cook for 3 minutes, stirring constantly. Stir in blueberries; reduce heat. Simmer 8-10 minutes or until berries have burst; add butter and stir until melted.

Ohio Berries!

In Ohio, Strawberries are in abundance in June. July is the peak month for blackberries and raspberries. Blueberries are in season from mid-July through mid-September.

Strawberry Parfait

"This is an old recipe from my wife's grandmother."
Jay & Liz Jozliwg—Burl Manor Bed & Breakfast, Lebanon

GRANOLA without raisins
VANILLA YOGURT
sm. STRAWBERRIES
BLUEBERRIES
GRANOLA without raisins
VANILLA YOGURT

In a parfait glass, layer ingredients in order given. Quick-freeze in the freezer for approximately 40 minutes. Add **1 lg. STRAWBERRY** to top when serving.

Breakfast Bread Pudding

"My parents purchased the farm I live on in 1943; the house was built in 1873! I have always lived here and come from generations of well-known cooks."

Patricia E. Jones—Warsaw

1/4 cup BUTTER, melted
3 EGGS, separated
2 cups MILK
1/2 tsp. DRY MUSTARD
1 can (4 oz.) chopped GREEN CHILES, drained
1/2 tsp. SALT
1/4 tsp. CAYENNE
9 slices BREAD, cut into 1/2-inch cubes
3 cups shredded SWISS CHEESE

In a bowl, combine butter, egg yolks, milk, mustard, chiles, salt and cayenne; mix well. Stir in bread and Swiss cheese. In a separate bowl, beat egg whites until soft peaks form; fold into bread mixture. Pour into a greased 9 x 9 baking dish. Cover and refrigerate overnight. Bake, uncovered, at 350° for 40-45 minutes or until knife inserted in the center comes out clean. Allow to set for 5 minutes before cutting.

Soups & Salads

Chilled Strawberry Soup

"This is a great treat during strawberry season."

Diane Roberts—Toledo

1 qt. STRAWBERRIES, cleaned and hulled
1/2 cup ORANGE JUICE
2 cups STRAWBERRY YOGURT
1/3 cup SUGAR
Pinch of SALT
Dash of NUTMEG
WHIPPED CREAM

Place strawberries in blender*, add orange juice and blend until smooth. In a bowl, combine yogurt, sugar, salt and nutmeg; stir well. Slowly add strawberry mixture, stirring well after each addition. Serve in bowls with a dollop of whipped cream on top.

*If desired, **TOFU** can be blended in with the strawberries for extra nutrition.

Ohio Tomato Soup

"When we have a surplus of tomatoes in the garden, I make a batch of this tasty soup!"

Dorothy A. Watkins—Portsmouth

8-10 ripe TOMATOES, peeled & chopped
1 qt. WATER
1 Tbsp. SUGAR
1 tsp. SALT
2 BAY LEAVES
4 WHOLE CLOVES
4 PEPPERCORNS
1-2 Tbsp. BUTTER
1 med. ONION, chopped
1-2 Tbsp. chopped PARSLEY
1 Tbsp. (heaping) FLOUR
SALT and PEPPER
1/4 tsp. BAKING SODA

In a soup pot, combine tomatoes, water, sugar, salt, bay leaves, cloves and peppercorns and bring to a boil. In a skillet, melt butter and sauté onion and parsley until onion is translucent; add flour and mix well. Add onion mixture to soup pot, stir, then season to taste. Stir in baking soda. Remove bay leaves before serving.

Lake Erie Fish-Corn Chowder

Ohio Sea Grant College Program, Columbus

1 lb. BACON, chopped
1 ONION, finely chopped
3 stalks CELERY, chopped
1 1/2 cups boned LAKE ERIE FISH FILLETS
FLOUR
1/2 lb. BUTTER or MARGARINE
2 cans (15 oz. ea.) CREAM STYLE CORN
1 qt. MILK
SALT and PEPPER to taste

In a skillet, fry bacon; remove and drain on paper towels. Add onion and celery to skillet and cook until golden brown; remove from skillet and set aside. Dredge fillets in flour and brown in bacon drippings. Discard drippings. Place all ingredients in a large kettle and simmer for 20 minutes. Season to taste with salt and pepper.

Broccoli-Cheese Soup

Rita Boose—Boose's Farm Market Inc., Norwalk

3/4 Tbsp. OIL or MARGARINE
3/4 cup chopped ONION
6 CHICKEN BOUILLON CUBES
6 cups WATER
1 pkg. (8 oz.) THIN NOODLES
2 pkgs. (10 oz. ea.) frozen CHOPPED
    BROCCOLI, thawed
1/4 tsp. GARLIC POWDER
1 tsp. SALT

6 cups MILK
1 lb. VELVEETA®, cubed

In a soup pot, heat oil and sauté onion for 3 minutes. Dissolve bouillon cubes in water; add to soup pot. Add noodles and simmer for 3 minutes. Add broccoli, garlic powder and salt and simmer for 4 minutes. Add milk and cheese and heat until cheese has melted.

Canton's Pro Football Hall of Fame

Visitors can experience the unique rotating Gameday Stadium Theatre. Hall highlights include films and memorabilia of professional football history. The Pro Football Hall of Fame Festival is held here every August.

Italian Vegetable Soup

"This soup is a family favorite!"

Mary A. Welch—Fremont

1 lb. GROUND BEEF
1 cup diced ONION
1 cup diced CELERY
1 cup sliced CARROTS
1 can (16 oz.) TOMATOES
1 can (15.5 oz.) RED KIDNEY
    BEANS, undrained
1 can (15 oz.) TOMATO SAUCE

2 cups WATER
5 tsp. BEEF BOUILLON
    GRANULES
1 Tbsp. dried PARSLEY
    FLAKES
1/2 tsp. OREGANO
1/4 tsp. PEPPER
1 cup ELBOW MACARONI

In a soup pot, brown beef and onion. Add vegetables, beans, tomato sauce, water, bouillon and seasonings. Bring soup to a boil; stir in macaroni. Reduce heat and cook for 30-45 minutes.

Amish Kidney Bean Salad

Molly Romano—Canton

2 cans (26 oz. ea.) RED KIDNEY
    BEANS, drained and rinsed
1/4 cup diced ONION

1/4 cup diced CELERY
1 cup SOUR CREAM
1 cup MAYONNAISE

In a bowl, combine kidney beans, onion and celery; set aside. Combine 2 cups of **Sweet & Sour Dressing** with sour cream and mayonnaise. Pour over bean mixture and stir well. Refrigerate overnight to allow flavors to blend.

Sweet & Sour Dressing

1 cup SUGAR
1 med. ONION, chopped
1/4 tsp. PEPPER
1 Tbsp. MAYONNAISE

1 tsp. CELERY SALT
1 cup SALAD OIL
3 tsp. MUSTARD
1/3 cup VINEGAR

In a bowl, combine all dressing ingredients together and beat well.

An Amish Barn Raising!

A barn raising is a community event for the Amish; entire families pitch in to help. The framing is usually completed before the noon-day meal—a feast prepared during the morning by the women—and the remainder completed in the afternoon. The bulk of the work is completed in one day!

 # Midwest Potato Salad

Brenda Hebron—West Lafayette

6 lg. POTATOES, boiled and cut
    into small pieces
6 HARD-BOILED EGGS, chopped
1 lg. ONION, chopped
2 Tbsp. PICKLE RELISH

1 1/2 cups MAYONNAISE
2 Tbsp. MUSTARD
2 Tbsp. PICKLE BRINE
    or VINEGAR

In a glass bowl, combine potatoes, eggs, onion and relish and mix well. In a separate bowl, combine mayonnaise, mustard and pickle brine and then stir into potato mixture. Chill until ready to serve.

Ohio Vegetable Salad

"My daughter gave me this recipe. We serve it at our family reunions."

Bea Lorenz—Fremont

1 can (14.5 oz.) FRENCH STYLE GREEN BEANS, drained
1 can (15 oz.) TINY GREEN PEAS, drained
1 can (15.25 oz.) WHITE SHOEPEG CORN, drained
1 jar (4 oz.) PIMENTOS, drained and diced
1/2 GREEN BELL PEPPER, finely diced
1 cup finely diced CELERY
1 cup finely diced ONION
1 tsp. SALT
1 tsp. PEPPER
1 Tbsp. WATER
3/4 cup VINEGAR
1/2 cup OIL
1 cup SUGAR

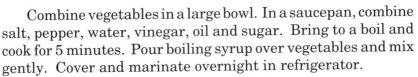

Combine vegetables in a large bowl. In a saucepan, combine salt, pepper, water, vinegar, oil and sugar. Bring to a boil and cook for 5 minutes. Pour boiling syrup over vegetables and mix gently. Cover and marinate overnight in refrigerator.

Note: Flavor improves when refrigerated for a day or two.

Midge's Potato Salad

"This is my own creation, developed while experimenting with different seasonings."

Midge Tucker—Marysville

1 lb. BACON
6-8 lg. WHITE POTATOES, boiled
1 bunch GREEN ONIONS, chopped
6 HARD-BOILED EGGS, chopped

MAYONNAISE
MUSTARD
SALT and PEPPER
SWEET RELISH

In a skillet, fry bacon until crisp; drain and crumble. In a large bowl, slightly mash potatoes (peel potatoes, if desired). Stir in bacon, onions and eggs. Fold in mayonnaise and seasonings to taste. Cover and refrigerate until ready to serve.

Mom's Seafood Salad

"This recipe is from my great-grandmother whose ancestors were from Germany."

Lynn Gilbert—Beavercreek

2 lbs. cooked SEAFOOD
1/2 cup FRENCH SALAD
    DRESSING
3-4 RED ONIONS, finely grated
1/2 cup finely grated CELERY
1 tsp. SALT
1/2 tsp. PEPPER

1 tsp. TABASCO®
1 tsp. WORCESTERSHIRE
    SAUCE
1 cup MAYONNAISE
2 HARD-BOILED EGGS,
    chopped

In a bowl, combine all ingredients except mayonnaise and eggs. Mix well and refrigerate for 30 minutes. When ready to serve, fold in mayonnaise and eggs.

Serves 6-8.

Did You Know?

Beginning in the 1830s and continuing into the 20th century, thousands of Germans immigrated to Ohio, clearing the land and draining the swamps for farming, establishing businesses and building churches. Today there are still many examples of German architecture in Ohio.

German Cole Slaw

"This is a great recipe that has been passed down through the years!."

Carole A. Damschroder—Gibsonburg

1 head CABBAGE, shredded
1 GREEN BELL PEPPER, diced
1 lg. ONION, diced
1 cup OIL

1 cup VINEGAR
1 1/2 cups SUGAR
2 tsp. SALT
2 Tbsp. CELERY SEED

In a bowl, combine cabbage, bell pepper and onion. In a saucepan, combine oil, vinegar, sugar, salt and celery seed and bring to a boil. Allow mixture to cool, then pour over cabbage mixture. Cover and refrigerate until ready to serve.

Pizza Salad

"This is a summer dish with a zesty flavor. It is a big hit at picnics and potluck dinners."

Kathleen C. White—Wintersville

1 pkg. (16 oz.) SPIRAL PASTA, cooked and drained
3-4 med. TOMATOES, seeded and diced
1 lb. CHEDDAR CHEESE, cubed
1-2 bunches GREEN ONIONS, sliced
3-4 oz. PEPPERONI, sliced

Dressing:
3/4 cup VEGETABLE OIL
2/3 cup grated PARMESAN CHEESE
1/2 cup RED WINE VINEGAR
2 tsp. OREGANO
1/2 tsp. GARLIC POWDER
1 tsp. SALT
1/4 tsp. PEPPER

In a bowl, combine pasta, tomatoes, cheese, onion and pepperoni. To prepare dressing: In a small bowl, combine all dressing ingredients, stir well. Pour dressing over pasta mixture; stir gently. Cover and refrigerate for several hours before serving.

Broccoli Slaw Salad

Kathryn Prusakiewicz—Sylvania

1 bag (16 oz.) BROCCOLI SLAW
2 pkgs. (3 oz. ea.) CHICKEN RAMEN® NOODLES, seasoning reserved
3/4 cup OIL
1/2 cup SUGAR
1/3 cup VINEGAR
1 cup SUNFLOWER SEEDS or 1/2 cup SUNFLOWER SEEDS and 1/2 cup chopped ENGLISH WALNUTS
1 cup slivered ALMONDS, roasted

Combine slaw and noodles together in a large bowl. In another bowl, combine oil, sugar, vinegar and reserved seasoning; mix well. Pour oil mixture over noodle mixture. Stir in sunflower seeds. Add almonds 1 hour before serving.

Note: Roast almonds at 350° for 5 minutes on a cookie sheet.

Macaroni Salad

"This is a favorite recipe I received from my aunt. My whole family loves this dish."

Mary Jo Goecke—Lakeview

2 pkgs. (16 oz. ea.) MACARONI
1 lg. GREEN BELL PEPPER, chopped
1 ONION, chopped
4 CARROTS, shredded

Dressing:
    1 can (14 oz.) SWEETENED CONDENSED MILK
    1 cup VINEGAR
    1 cup SUGAR
    2 cups MIRACLE WHIP® or MAYONNAISE
    1 tsp. SALT
    1/4 tsp. PEPPER

Cook macaroni according to package directions; drain and allow to cool. In a bowl, combine all vegetables and mix well. In another bowl, combine all dressing ingredients and mix well. Add macaroni to vegetables. Stir in dressing mixture and mix thoroughly. Chill at least 4 hours before serving.

Punajuurisalaattii

(Beet Salad)

"This is a delicious Finnish side dish very similar to a cranberry sauce. It has a beautiful red-purple color. Northwest Ohio has a rich and diverse ethnic blend. The whole summer can be spent attending one ethnic festival after another–German, Irish, Hungarian, Polish, Hispanic, African-American, Greek and many others."

Carol Savolaine—Sylvania

4 cups peeled, diced and
    cooked BEETS
1 Tbsp. VINEGAR
1/4 cup HEAVY CREAM

1/4 cup MAYONNAISE
1 1/2 tsp. HORSERADISH
Dash of SALT

Place beets in a bowl. Combine remaining ingredients and mix well. Pour over beets and stir gently. Chill at least 1 hour.

Springtime Salad

"This is a favorite during strawberry season!"

Doris A. Bendele—Ottawa

1 pkg. (3 oz.) STRAWBERRY JELL-O®
1 cup HOT WATER
1 cup sliced fresh STRAWBERRIES
1 cup MINIATURE MARSHMALLOWS
1/2 cup chopped NUTS
3/4 cup CRUSHED PINEAPPLE
1 cup WHIPPING CREAM or EVAPORATED MILK
2 Tbsp. LEMON JUICE

In a mixing bowl, dissolve Jell-O in hot water; allow to cool 15-20 minutes. Stir in strawberries, marshmallows, nuts and pineapple. Chill whipping cream in refrigerator tray for 15-20 minutes or until soft crystals form. In a bowl, whip cream for 1 minute or until stiff; add lemon juice and whip until very stiff. Fold Jell-O mixture into whipped cream. Spoon into a 1 1/2-quart mold or 6 individual molds. Chill 1-2 hours.

Mom's Party Cherry Salad

"This was our special 'birthday salad' when I was a child."

Betty Bridenstine—West Salem

1 can (16 oz.) DARK CHERRIES
1 can (20 oz.) PINEAPPLE CHUNKS
1/3 cup LEMON JUICE
WATER
1 pkg. (6 oz.) CHERRY JELL-O®
3 Tbsp. LIGHT CREAM
3 oz. CREAM CHEESE, softened
1/2 cup chopped WALNUTS

In a large saucepan, combine juice from cherries and pineapple; add lemon juice and enough water to equal 3 1/2 cups. Bring mixture to a boil, add Jell-O and stir until dissolved. Divide liquid in half. Chill 1 portion until partially set; stir in pineapple. Pour into a 13 x 9 glass dish and chill until firm. In a small bowl, blend cream and cream cheese together; spread over firm Jell-O and refrigerate. Chill remaining half of Jell-O to syrup consistency; add walnuts and cherries. Pour over cream cheese mixture and chill until firm.

Sugar Free Rhubarb-Strawberry Salad

"We love to use the rhubarb from our Ohio garden to make this delicious salad."

Harriet Grail—Columbus

3 cups diced RHUBARB
1 pt. STRAWBERRIES, hulled and halved
1 cup WATER
1 pkg. (3 oz.) STRAWBERRY, CHERRY, or RASPBERRY
** SUGAR FREE JELL-O®**
SUGAR SUBSTITUTE

In a saucepan, combine rhubarb, strawberries and water; bring to a boil. Reduce heat and stir in Jell-O. Cook on low heat until rhubarb is tender. Sweeten to taste with sugar substitute. Pour into a glass casserole or serving dish. Chill until firm.

Strawberry-Pretzel Salad

"My sister-in-law, Mary, gave me this recipe. It's one of my husband's favorites."

Brenda Allen Keller—Lima

2 cups crushed PRETZELS
3/4 cup MARGARINE, melted
1 cup + 3 tsp. SUGAR, divided
1 pkg. (8 oz.) CREAM CHEESE,
** softened**
1 ctn. (8 oz.) COOL WHIP® TOPPING
2 pkgs. (3 oz. ea.) STRAWBERRY JELL-O®
2 cups BOILING WATER
2 pkgs. (10 oz. ea.) frozen STRAWBERRIES, sweetened

In a bowl, mix pretzels, margarine and 3 teaspoons sugar together; spread in a 13 x 9 pan. Bake at 400° for 8 minutes; allow to cool. In a bowl, mix cream cheese, remaining sugar and Cool Whip together; spread mixture over pretzels. Dissolve Jell-O in water and stir in strawberries. Let stand for 5-10 minutes or until partially set. Pour over cream cheese mixture. Refrigerate for several hours or overnight.

Main Dishes

Homemade Hungarian Chicken Paprika

"This is a favorite Hungarian recipe that has been passed down from my great-grandmother, Elizabeth Terebesi."

Christine Marie Pozega—Lorain

1 Tbsp. VEGETABLE OIL
1 sm. ONION, diced
8-10 pieces boneless, skinless CHICKEN
3-4 Tbsp. PAPRIKA
2 ctns. (16 oz. ea.) SOUR CREAM
1/2 tsp. SALT
1/2 tsp. PEPPER
1 can (10.75 oz.) CREAM OF CELERY SOUP
1 can (10.75 oz.) CREAM OF CHICKEN SOUP

Heat oil in a skillet and sauté onion until translucent. Add chicken and sprinkle with paprika. Stir in sour cream, salt and pepper. In a bowl, combine soups and stir well; add to chicken mixture. Simmer for 1-2 hours, or until chicken is tender.

Note: Add homemade dumplings or spaetzle noodles if desired.

Margaret's Sloppy Joes

"My mother has made this for as long as I can remember. She created the recipe after reading numerous variations of sloppy joe recipes in cookbooks and talking to family and friends."

Sue Perine O'Reilly—Hamilton

1-1 1/2 lbs. GROUND BEEF	1 Tbsp. WORCESTERSHIRE
1/2-1 sm. ONION, chopped	SAUCE
1/4 tsp. CELERY SEED, optional	1/2 tsp. CHILI POWDER
1 Tbsp. SWEET PICKLE JUICE	1/2 GREEN BELL PEPPER,
3/4 cup KETCHUP	chopped
3 Tbsp. BROWN SUGAR	SALT and PEPPER
1/2-1 Tbsp. MUSTARD	HAMBURGER BUNS

In a skillet, combine beef, onion and celery seed. Sauté until beef is browned; drain. Stir in remaining ingredients (except buns), seasoning with salt and pepper to taste. Simmer, uncovered, for approximately 1 hour. Continue cooking over low heat until desired consistency. Serve on hamburger buns.

Note: Vinegar or water can be substituted for sweet pickle juice. Also, thin sauce with tomato juice or water if needed.

Serves 8-10.

Baked Beef Stew

"My sister-in-law gave me this recipe. It's great for busy days!"

Carol Hefner—Harrod

2 lbs. BEEF CUBES	2 Tbsp. (heaping) INSTANT
6 CARROTS, sliced	TAPIOCA
3 ONIONS, chopped	2 POTATOES, peeled and
1 cup chopped CELERY	quartered
1 Tbsp. SUGAR	1 cup BREAD CRUMBS
2 cups whole TOMATOES	

Combine all ingredients, except for bread crumbs in a roasting pan. Sprinkle bread crumbs on top. Bake at 250° for 5 hours.

Cincinnati "5-Way" Chili

Karen Anderson—Cincinnati

2 lbs. GROUND BEEF
4 med. ONIONS, chopped
1 clove GARLIC, minced
2 tsp. VINEGAR
1 can (12 oz.) TOMATO PASTE
2-3 Tbsp. CHILI POWDER
3 tsp. CINNAMON

1 tsp. TABASCO®
1/2 oz. BITTER CHOCOLATE
   (or 1 Tbsp. COCOA POWDER)
2 dashes WORCESTERSHIRE
   SAUCE
1 qt. WATER
1 1/2 tsp. SALT

Spice Bag:
   4 DRY PEPPERS
   35 WHOLE ALLSPICE
   5 BAY LEAVES

Serve with:
   Cooked SPAGHETTI
   Shredded SHARP CHEDDAR
      CHEESE

Chopped ONIONS
Cooked KIDNEY BEANS
OYSTER CRACKERS

Sauté beef, onions and garlic. Add remaining ingredients including spice bag. Simmer, partially covered for one hour. Remove spice bag.

To serve, assemble by layers on serving plates:
1. Hot spaghetti
2. Chili
3. Cheese
4. Onions
5. Kidney beans

Top with oyster crackers.

Serves 6-8.

Did You Know?

Cincinnati chili was created in 1922 by a Macedonian immigrant, Athenas Kiradjieff. He settled in Cincinnati, opened a hot dog stand called the Empress and began creating chili with Middle Eastern spices.

Grandma Ratliff's Chicken & Dumplings

"My grandparents settled in southern Ohio in 1924. They purchased land, cleared it and built their home from the timber on the property. They raised cows and chickens and had a garden, an orchard and grew many kinds of berries. Each Sunday morning my grandmother would prepare her special chicken recipe."

Donna Hacker—Ironton

1 (5 lb.) STEWING CHICKEN   **1 cup MILK**
1 tsp. SALT   **WATER**

Place whole chicken in a large soup kettle and cover with water; add salt. Cook over low heat for approximately 3 hours or until meat is tender; remove chicken, reserving broth, and let chicken cool; debone. Heat chicken broth over medium heat; add milk and enough water to equal 2 gallons, bring to a boil. Carefully drop dumpling dough by large spoonfuls into boiling broth and cook for 20 minutes, stirring frequently. Reduce heat to low, add chicken back to kettle and continue to cook for 5-10 minutes or until broth thickens into a gravy.

Serves 8-10.

Grandma's Dumplings

4 cups SELF-RISING FLOUR   **12 drops YELLOW FOOD**
3 cups MILK   **COLORING**
1 cup CHICKEN BROTH   **SALT and PEPPER**
1/4 cup COOKING OIL

In a mixing bowl, combine all ingredients, seasoning with salt and pepper to taste. Mix well and then let rise for 5 minutes.

Ohio's Shoreline

Ohio has 312 miles of shoreline along Lake Erie, from Conneaut in the east to Toledo in the west. It includes 53 miles along Sandusky Bay and 66 miles along offshore islands.

Best Stuffed Peppers

"Bell peppers grow in abundance in Ohio gardens and have always been a favorite of my family. I have developed this recipe over the years and this is my best combination yet."

Carolyn Robison—Bluffton

1 can (10.75 oz.) TOMATO SOUP
1 TOMATO, chopped
1 can (14.5 oz.) diced TOMATOES or TOMATOES with CHILES
1 lb. GROUND BEEF
1/2 cup MINUTE® RICE
1 sm. ONION, chopped
1 EGG, beaten
1 Tbsp. WORCESTERSHIRE SAUCE
SALT and PEPPER
3 GREEN BELL PEPPERS, halved and seeded
2 cups shredded CHEDDAR CHEESE

In a bowl, combine soup, fresh and canned tomatoes. In another bowl, combine beef, rice, onion, egg, Worcestershire sauce and 1/2 of the tomato mixture. Season with salt and pepper to taste. Fill bell pepper halves with beef mixture and place in a greased casserole dish. Pour remaining tomato mixture over top. Bake, covered, at 350° for 1 1/2 hours. During the last 20 minutes of baking time, sprinkle with cheese and continue to bake, uncovered, until done.

Ham Loaf

"This is a variation of a recipe from an old cookbook."

Eleanor Williams—Gibsonburg

1 lb. GROUND HAM
1 lb. GROUND PORK
1 cup TOMATO JUICE
1 cup CRACKER CRUMBS

1 EGG, beaten
2 tsp. SUGAR
1 cup MILK

Mix all ingredients together in a bowl. Press lightly into a 9 x 5 loaf pan. Bake at 300° for 2 hours.

Note: Loaf can be topped with **PINEAPPLE SLICES** and sprinkled with **BROWN SUGAR** and **CLOVES** before baking.

Lake Erie Drum Au Gratin

Ohio Sea Grant College Program, Columbus

2 lbs. DRUM FILLETS	2 ONIONS, sliced
2 Tbsp. BUTTER, melted	1/2 cup SOUR CREAM
SALT and PEPPER to taste	5 Tbsp. grated CHEESE
1/2 lb. MUSHROOMS, thinly sliced	1 Tbsp. BREAD CRUMBS

Preheat oven to 400°. Place fillets in a buttered 13 x 9 baking dish and sprinkle with butter. Bake for 10 minutes. In a skillet, sauté mushrooms and onions until onions are translucent. Add salt and pepper and stir. Layer mushroom mixture on top of fillets. Pour sour cream over all and sprinkle with cheese and bread crumbs. Bake for 10 minutes or until fish flakes easily.

Serves 6.

Lake Erie, Recovered!

Over 30 years ago, the Cuyahoga River caught fire and Lake Erie became the "poster child" for this country's pollution problems. With pollution abatement and improvements in natural resources management, Lake Erie is once again a thriving resource and provides abundant fishing and recreational opportunities.

Rosemary Pork Chops

This recipe is from the "I'll cook when pigs fly...and they do in Cincinnati" cookbook.

Junior League of Cincinnati

Marinade:

1/4 cup DIJON MUSTARD	3 Tbsp. fresh ROSEMARY
1/4 cup BALSAMIC VINEGAR	3/4 tsp. SALT
1/4 cup LEMON JUICE	1 tsp. PEPPER
6 cloves GARLIC, minced	1/2 cup OLIVE OIL

8 PORK CHOPS

In a bowl, thoroughly combine marinade ingredients. Place pork chops in a glass or ceramic baking dish and cover with marinade. Marinate for 2 hours in the refrigerator. Drain marinade and grill chops until done.

Scott's Special Casserole

"This is a variation of my mother's casserole."

Scott Hilton—Columbus

2 Tbsp. BUTTER
1 GREEN BELL PEPPER, chopped
1 RED BELL PEPPER, chopped
1 lg. YELLOW ONION, chopped
2 cans (4.5 oz. ea.) sliced MUSHROOMS or
    1 lb. fresh MUSHROOMS, sliced
1 lb. GROUND BEEF
1 lb. GROUND SAGE SAUSAGE
1 1/2 lbs. PASTA
1-2 jars (32 oz. ea.) SPAGHETTI SAUCE
1/2 lb. COLBY-JACK CHEESE, grated

In a skillet, melt butter and sauté bell peppers, onion and mushrooms for 3-4 minutes; remove from skillet and set aside. Place beef and sausage in skillet and brown; drain. In a large soup pot, cook pasta according to package directions; drain well. Combine vegetable mixture, meat mixture and pasta and toss gently to mix. Add sauce and cheese; stir until well-mixed and cheese has melted.

Eggplant Parmesan

"I have always enjoyed cooking and love to collect cookbooks."

Nancy E. Wood—Columbus

1 med. EGGPLANT
1 tsp. SALT
1/2 cup FLOUR
1/2 cup MARGARINE
1 lb. GROUND CHUCK

2 cups SPAGHETTI SAUCE
2 cups grated MOZZARELLA
    CHEESE
1/4 cup PARMESAN CHEESE

Peel eggplant and thinly slice. Place salt and flour in a plastic bag, add eggplant and shake well to coat. In a skillet, melt margarine, add eggplant and brown on both sides; remove from skillet and place in a 13 x 9 casserole dish. Add beef to skillet and cook until browned; drain. Layer top of eggplant with meat, then spaghetti sauce, mozzarella and Parmesan cheese. Bake, uncovered, at 350° for 30 minutes.

Steak & Mushrooms

"This is one of the few recipes I have from my Grandma Werling."

Lynn Ungru—Harrison

1 ROUND STEAK	1 can (10.75 oz.) CREAM
MEAT TENDERIZER	OF MUSHROOM SOUP
4 Tbsp. FLOUR	1 Tbsp. HORSERADISH
VEGETABLE OIL	SALT and PEPPER
1/2 cup WATER	Cooked RICE

Sprinkle steak with meat tenderizer, cut into bite-size pieces and dredge in flour to coat. Heat a small amount of oil in a heavy iron skillet, add steak and cook until browned; remove from skillet. Mix 2 tablespoons flour and water and stir into drippings in skillet. Add soup and horseradish and mix until smooth, adding more water if needed. Season with salt and pepper to taste. Return steak to skillet, cover and simmer for 1 hour, stirring often. Serve over rice.

Play Ball!
In 1869, the Cincinnati Red Stockings became the first professional baseball team in America.

To-Die-For Scallops

"This is my original creation, born of a love for seafood. It is incredibly delicious."

Cindy McPherson—Fremont

1 stick BUTTER or MARGARINE	1/2 cup chopped GREEN
3 Tbsp. SOY SAUCE	ONIONS
1 1/2 tsp. GARLIC POWDER	1/2-3/4 cup CRACKER
3 Tbsp. LEMON JUICE	CRUMBS
1 lb. TINY SCALLOPS	LEMON SLICES

Melt butter in a skillet and add soy sauce, garlic powder, lemon juice and scallops. Cook over medium heat for 15 minutes. During the last 5 minutes of cooking time, add green onions. When done, add enough cracker crumbs to absorb juice. Serve with lemon slices on the side.

Hamburger Pie

"This is quick and easy to make. Tomatoes are a major agricultural crop in our area of Ohio. Mercer County has two canneries which are very busy during our harvest season."

Rosemary L. Hagar—Celina

1 lb. GROUND BEEF
1/2 cup chopped ONION
1/2 tsp. SALT
Dash of PEPPER
1 can (14.5 oz.) GREEN
 BEANS, drained

1 can (10.75 oz.) TOMATO
 SOUP
5 med. POTATOES, peeled and
 and boiled
1/2 cup shredded AMERICAN
 CHEESE

In a skillet, brown beef and onion; add salt and pepper. Stir in beans and soup. Pour mixture into a greased 1 1/2-quart casserole dish. Mash potatoes and spoon in mounds over meat mixture; sprinkle with cheese. Bake at 350° for 25-30 minutes.

Oven-Barbecued Ribs

"Ohio has many farms that provide fresh meat to Ohio cooks. A friend of mine shared this recipe with me many years ago."

Helen Nilan—Washington Court House

4 lbs. boneless SPARERIBS
GARLIC SALT

Basting Sauce:
1/2 cup VINEGAR
1 tsp. SALT
1 tsp. DRY MUSTARD
2 tsp. CELERY SEED
1/4 cup SUGAR

1 1/2 tsp. CHILI POWDER
 or 1/4 tsp. CAYENNE
1 tsp. PAPRIKA
1/2 tsp. PEPPER
1 cup WATER

Season both sides of ribs with garlic salt to taste. In a bowl, combine sauce ingredients and mix well. Place ribs in a roasting pan and pour sauce over top. Bake, covered, at 325° for 2 1/2 hours. Baste ribs with sauce every 30-40 minutes while baking.

What's in a Name?

The city of Washington Court House is the seat of Fayette County. In the late 1820s, Washington added "Court House" to its name to distinguish it from four other Washingtons in Ohio.

Old Time Chicken & Noodles

"This is an old Amish recipe. The homemade noodles are what makes it the best!"

Roy Hatten—Franklin Furnace

**1 (3-4 lb.) CHICKEN
3 CHICKEN BOUILLON CUBES
SALT and PEPPER**

Place chicken in a soup kettle and cover with water. Cook until tender; remove and allow to cool before deboning. Add bouillon cubes for a rich flavor. Stir ***Homemade Noodles*** into broth and cook until tender. Return chicken to kettle and season with salt and pepper to taste.

Homemade Noodles

**6 EGG YOLKS   1/2 tsp. SALT
6 Tbsp. WATER   2 1/2 cups FLOUR**

In a bowl, beat egg yolks and water together. Stir in salt and enough flour to make a very stiff, yet workable dough. Divide dough into four parts. Roll each part out as thin as possible and lay each on a separate cloth to dry. When dough is no longer sticky, stack and cut lengthwise into thin strips; cut strips into 2-inch pieces.

Note: If noodles are not going to be cooked right away, they can be dried completely and stored in an airtight container.

The Ohio River

The Ohio River is one of the chief rivers of North America. It flows more than 450 miles along Ohio's southern and southeastern borders. The northern bank of the river forms the state boundary.

Dilled Salmon Patties

Edie Jeanneret—Wapakoneta

1 can (16 oz.) SALMON
2 Tbsp. BUTTER or MARGARINE
1/2 cup chopped ONION
2/3 cup FINE BREAD CRUMBS, divided
2 EGGS, beaten
1 tsp. dried DILL WEED
1/2 tsp. DRY MUSTARD or 1 tsp. MUSTARD
2 Tbsp. COOKING OIL or SHORTENING

Drain salmon, reserving 2 tablespoons of liquid; discard bones and skin, then flake. In a skillet, melt butter and sauté onion until translucent; remove from heat. Add reserved liquid from salmon, 1/3 cup of the bread crumbs, eggs, dill weed, mustard and salmon; mix well. Shape into 4 patties and coat with remaining bread crumbs. In a skillet, heat oil and cook patties over medium heat for 3 minutes or until browned; turn and brown the other side. Serve with lemon wedges.

Tangy Baked Chicken

"I entered this recipe in the Ohio Chicken Cooking Contest in Dayton. It was one of 16 chosen in the Grand Winner Category."

Grace E. Baum—Bellevue

1 (3 lb.) CHICKEN, cut into pieces

Marinade:
1 cup LEMON-LIME SODA   1 tsp. ROSEMARY
1 1/2 tsp. SEASONED SALT   1 tsp. SALT
1/2 cup CORN OIL   1/2 tsp. PEPPER
1 med. ONION, diced

Arrange chicken in a deep baking dish. In a bowl, thoroughly combine all marinade ingredients. Pour marinade over chicken. Cover and refrigerate for 3 hours, turning twice. Remove chicken from marinade and place in a shallow baking pan. Bake at 425° for 30-45 minutes, basting often with marinade.

Salmon Quiche

"I really enjoy serving this at our Bed & Breakfast."
Maryann & Hank Burwinkel—The Empty Nest Bed & Breakfast,
Norwood

Crust:

1 cup FLOUR	1/4 cup chopped ALMONDS
2/3 cup shredded SHARP CHEDDAR CHEESE	1/4 tsp. PAPRIKA
	1/3 cup VEGETABLE OIL

Filling:

1 can (14.75 oz.) SALMON, drained, liquid reserved	1/2 cup shredded SHARP CHEDDAR CHEESE
3 EGGS, beaten	1 Tbsp. grated ONION
1 cup SOUR CREAM	1/2 tsp. dried DILL WEED
1/4 cup MAYONNAISE	3 drops HOT PEPPER SAUCE

To prepare crust: In a bowl, combine flour, cheese, almonds and paprika; stir in oil. Set aside 1/4 cup of crust mixture. Press remaining mixture onto the bottom and up the sides of a 9-inch pie pan or quiche dish. Bake crust at 400° for 10 minutes. Remove from oven and reduce oven temperature to 325°. To prepare filling: Flake salmon, remove and discard bones and skin; set aside. Measure reserved liquid from salmon and add enough water to equal 1/2 cup. In a bowl, blend salmon liquid, eggs, sour cream and mayonnaise. Stir in salmon, cheese, onion, dill weed and hot pepper sauce. Spoon filling into crust; sprinkle with reserved crust mixture. Bake at 325° for 45 minutes or until firm and knife inserted in center comes out clean. Serve hot or cold or freeze and bake when needed.

Ohio's Land Regions

During the Ice Age, several glaciers moved across what is now Ohio except the southeastern part. The glaciers helped create the state's four regions:
- *Great Lakes Plains*
- *Till Plains*
- *Appalachian Plateau*
- *Bluegrass Region*

Baked Steak Sandwiches

"There never seems to be any leftovers with these!"

Connie Combs—Beavercreek

1 lg. FLANK STEAK
2 lg. TOMATOES, quartered
1 lg. GREEN BELL PEPPER, sliced into thin rings
1 lg. BERMUDA ONION, sliced into thin rings
1 can (4.5 oz.) WHOLE BUTTON MUSHROOMS, drained
2 Tbsp. BUTTER, cut into pieces
3 Tbsp. CHILI SAUCE
3 Tbsp. KETCHUP
1 Tbsp. WORCESTERSHIRE SAUCE
HOAGIE BUNS cut into 2-inch sections or other SMALL BUNS

Preheat oven to 350°. Place steak in a shallow pan. Cover with tomatoes, bell pepper, onion and mushrooms, then dot with butter. In a bowl, combine chili sauce, ketchup and worcestershire sauce; mix well. Pour over top of vegetables. Place pan in oven and bake, uncovered, for 45 minutes or until meat is tender. Thinly slice steak cross-grain. Serve on buns.

Lake Erie Potato-Fried Fish

Ohio Sea Grant College Program, Columbus

1 1/2 lbs. WHITE BASS, YELLOW PERCH or other FILLETS
1 tsp. SALT
1/4 tsp. PEPPER
1 EGG, beaten
1 Tbsp. WATER
1 cup INSTANT MASHED POTATOES
1 pkg (.06 oz.) ONION or ITALIAN SALAD
    DRESSING MIX
COOKING OIL

Sprinkle fish fillets with salt and pepper. In a bowl, beat together egg and water. In another bowl, combine potato flakes and dressing mix. Dip fish into egg mixture to coat then dredge in potato flake mixture. Heat 1/8-inch oil in a skillet. Add fish and over moderate heat, fry for 4-5 minutes per side. Drain on paper towels.

Lasagna

"My husband likes to eat a lot of meat and we both love pepperoni. He says this is the best lasagna he has ever tasted."
Mary Cowger—Cowger House Bed & Breakfast & Country Inn, Zoar

1 pkg. (16 oz.) LASAGNA NOODLES

Meat Sauce:

1 1/2 lbs. GROUND CHUCK	1 tsp. GARLIC POWDER
1/2 lb. PEPPERONI, sliced	2 BAY LEAVES
2 tsp. ITALIAN SEASONING	1 can (12 oz.) TOMATO PASTE
1-2 Tbsp. SUGAR	1 can (12 oz.) WATER

Cheese Filling:

4 cups grated MOZZARELLA CHEESE	1 tsp. PARSLEY FLAKES
1 lb. RICOTTA CHEESE	1/8 tsp. GARLIC POWDER
2 EGGS	1 tsp. ITALIAN SEASONING

Cook noodles according to package directions. To prepare meat sauce: In a skillet, cook beef until browned, then add remaining sauce ingredients and heat thoroughly. Remove bay leaves. To prepare filling: In a bowl, combine 1 3/4 cups mozzarella cheese and remaining filling ingredients; mix well. In a baking dish, arrange a layer of noodles, sauce and cheese filling; repeat layer. Top with a single layer of noodles and sprinkle remaining mozzarella cheese on top. Bake at 350° for 40 minutes.

Indian Earthworks in Ohio

Notable earthworks to be found in Ohio include: The Newark Earthworks(a), at Newark, has two areas, an octagonal area that encloses about 50 acres and circular walls that enclose about 20 acres. Fort Hill(b), near Bainbridge, is a 1,200-acre area with a great walled enclosure on a high hill. Fort Ancient(c), near Lebanon, is the largest hilltop earth structure in the U.S. Its walls, more than 20 feet high and 3 miles long, enclose over 100 acres.

Bubble & Squeak

"My mother's Welsh friend gave her this recipe. It is delicious and great fun to make. This is wonderful when served with salad or fruit."

Shirley Baston—The Blue Pencil, Fremont

3 POTATOES, unpeeled
4 cups chopped CABBAGE, blanched
1/2 med. ONION, chopped
1 ZUCCHINI, grated
1/4 cup chopped HAM
3 slices BACON, browned and crumbled, drippings reserved
PEPPER

In a saucepan, boil potatoes until tender; drain. Slightly mash potatoes, then combine with remaining ingredients, except for bacon drippings, seasoning with pepper to taste. In a non-stick skillet, heat bacon drippings, then press potato mixture into skillet. Cook over medium heat for 1/2 hour or until golden brown; do not stir. Invert onto a plate to serve.

Sauerkraut & Pork Chops

"A co-worker gave me this easy and delicious recipe."

Pamela S. Furlong—Greenville

4 PORK CHOPS
SALT and PEPPER
2 Tbsp. OIL
1 jar (32 oz.) SAUERKRAUT WITH CARAWAY SEED
2 Tbsp. BROWN SUGAR
4 POTATOES, peeled and halved
2 Tbsp. BUTTER or MARGARINE
1/4 cup WATER

Lightly season pork chops with salt and pepper. In a skillet, heat oil and lightly brown pork chops. Drain sauerkraut thoroughly and place in a bowl, add brown sugar and mix well. Place potatoes in bottom of a 2-quart casserole dish. Spread sauerkraut mixture over potatoes. Place pork chops on top and dot with butter. Add water and cover. Bake at 325° for 3 hours.

Serves 2.

Geschnetzeltes
(Guh-shnet-sel-tis)

This Swiss Julienne of Veal recipe is from the "I'll cook when pigs fly...and they do in Cincinnati" cookbook.

Junior League of Cincinnati

2 lbs. VEAL CUTLETS, cut 1/2-inch thick
SALT and PEPPER to taste
PAPRIKA, to taste
3 Tbsp. BUTTER or MARGARINE
2 Tbsp. chopped GREEN ONION
3 Tbsp. ALL-PURPOSE FLOUR
1 cup WHIPPING CREAM
1/2 cup DRY WHITE WINE
1 cup sliced MUSHROOMS, optional
1/4 cup BRANDY

Place each cutlet between waxed paper sheets and using a mallet, pound to 1/4-inch thickness. Season to taste with salt, pepper and paprika. Cut each cutlet into 1 1/2 x 1/4-inch strips. In a large skillet, melt butter and sauté onions until softened. Add veal strips and cook over medium-high heat for about 4 minutes or until no longer pink. Remove veal. Stir flour into pan drippings and cook, stirring until bubbly. Gradually blend in cream and wine. Cook, stirring often, until thickened and smooth. Add mushrooms. Just before serving, add veal to sauce in skillet or chafing dish. Cook, stirring frequently, for about 5 minutes. Heat brandy until warm to touch. Ignite and pour over veal in sauce. Stir until flame expires and serve.

Serves 6.

Serpent Mound State Memorial

One of the few effigy mounds in Ohio, this prehistoric structure is one of the best-known in the world. The mound represents a giant un-coiling snake. It has seven deep curves, aver-ages 3 feet in height and is over 1,330 feet long. The mound lies on a plateau overlooking the valley of Brush Creek in Adams County.

Side Dishes

Spinach Tomatofeller

"In the summer we have an abundance of tomatoes. This is a nice party recipe that makes a good presentation."

Billi Schmidt—Dayton

2 pkgs. (10 oz. ea.) frozen chopped SPINACH
1/4 cup DRIED BREAD CRUMBS
1/4 cup minced GREEN ONIONS
2 EGGS, beaten
4 Tbsp. BUTTER, melted
1/4 cup PARMESAN CHEESE
1/2 tsp. minced GARLIC
1/2 tsp. minced fresh THYME
1/8 tsp. freshly ground BLACK PEPPER
1/4 tsp. SALT
8 slices (1/4-inch thick) TOMATO
1 PIMENTO, thinly sliced

Preheat oven to 350°. Cook spinach according to package directions; drain. Combine spinach with all remaining ingredients, except for tomato and pimento and mix well. Arrange tomato slices on the bottom of a 2-quart glass baking dish. Sprinkle with additional salt and pepper to taste. Spoon 1/4 cup spinach mixture onto each tomato slice and shape into a dome. Bake for 15 minutes or until set and heated through. Garnish with pimento slices.

Freezer Pickles

"My sister-in-law shared this recipe with me. These pickles are a refreshing treat during winter when snow covers the ground."

Carole A. Damschroder—Gibsonburg

7 cups thinly sliced CUCUMBERS
1 cup chopped ONION
1 cup chopped GREEN BELL PEPPER
2 cups SUGAR
1 tsp. CELERY SEED
1 1/2 tsp. SALT
1 cup WHITE VINEGAR

Combine all ingredients in a glass or ceramic bowl; allow to stand for 4 hours. Spoon mixture into small containers. Freeze.

Sweet Potato Casserole

"This dish is always requested at our church dinners, reunions and holiday dinners. It not only tastes good but looks scrumptious, too."

Marianne Lucas—West Portsmouth

3 cups mashed SWEET POTATOES
1 cup SUGAR
1/2 cup BUTTER, melted
2 EGGS
1 tsp. VANILLA
1/3 cup MILK

Topping:
  1/2 cup packed BROWN SUGAR
  1/4 cup FLOUR
  2 1/2 Tbsp. melted BUTTER
  1/2 cup chopped PECANS

In a bowl, beat sweet potatoes, sugar, butter, eggs, vanilla and milk until blended. Pour into a 2-quart casserole dish. To prepare topping: In a bowl, combine all topping ingredients and mix well; sprinkle on casserole. Bake at 350° for 25 minutes.

Dress Up Vegetables

"A very good friend gave me this recipe and it is delicious!"

Donna C. Richards—Lima

1 1/2 cups WATER
1 sm. ONION, diced
1/2 stick MARGARINE
1 pkg. (16 oz.) frozen MIXED VEGETABLES, thawed
2/3 cup MINUTE® RICE
1 can (10.75 oz.) CREAM OF MUSHROOM SOUP
2 cups shredded CHEDDAR CHEESE
1 can (8 oz.) sliced WATER CHESTNUTS
1/2 cup BREAD CRUMBS

In a saucepan, bring water to a boil and add onion and margarine. Stir in remaining ingredients except bread crumbs. Pour mixture into a 13 x 9 casserole dish and sprinkle top with bread crumbs. Bake at 350° for 45 minutes.

Cleveland Rocks! So does Cincinnati!

Ohio cities have served as the setting for television shows, including Cleveland for "The Drew Carey Show" and Cincinnati for "WKRP in Cincinnati."

Mashed Potato Stuffing

"This makes a very tasty side dish"

Faye Bridenstine—West Salem

2 loaves BREAD, torn
  into small pieces
1 stick BUTTER
1 med. ONION, diced
1 stalk CELERY, diced
1 CARROT, diced
5 EGG YOLKS

1 cup MASHED POTATOES
1 tsp. BAKING POWDER
1 1/2 tsp. POULTRY
  SEASONING
1 tsp. SALT
3/4 tsp. PEPPER
2 cups CHICKEN BROTH

Place bread in a casserole dish. In a skillet, melt butter and sauté onion, celery and carrot until crisp-tender. Pour mixture over bread. In a bowl, beat egg yolks; add potatoes, baking powder, poultry seasoning, salt and pepper and mix thoroughly. Pour egg mixture over bread and vegetables. Add chicken broth and mix lightly. Bake at 325° for 1 hour.

Turkey Stuffing

"Thanksgiving was always special when I was growing up. Early in the morning, I'd awaken to the smell of sage and sautéed onions and celery. This stuffing recipe is wonderful!"

Beth Loughner—Columbus

3 Tbsp. BUTTER
2 med. ONIONS, diced
2 stalks CELERY, diced
1 loaf BREAD, dried and cubed
1/2 tsp. PEPPER
1/2 tsp. SALT
2 Tbsp. SAGE
1 can (14.5 oz.) CHICKEN BROTH

In a skillet, melt butter and sauté onion and celery until onion is translucent. In another bowl, combine bread, pepper, salt and sage; toss lightly; add onions and celery and stir. Pour chicken broth slowly over bread mixture and stir to mix well. Place stuffing in a 3-quart casserole dish. Bake at 350° for 45-60 minutes.

Note: This recipe makes enough to loosely stuff a 12 lb. turkey.

Homemade Sauerkraut

"I have lived in the country all of my life and have always had a garden. Granny always canned food from our garden. One of my favorites was sauerkraut!"

Roy Hatten—Franklin Furnace

Shred **1 head of CABBAGE** into 1/8-inch wide strips and pack tightly into hot, sterilized quart jars. Add **1 1/2 Tsp. PICKLNG SALT** to each. Fill each jar with **BOILING WATER** to within 1/2-inch from top. Immediately seal jars tightly by hand. Set jars in a pan to catch any leakage during fermenting process. Let set for 4-6 weeks before using.

Note: The brine may look milky, especially on the bottom of the jars, but this will not affect the sauerkraut.

Elegant
Celery Casserole

"Nearby Summit County grows acres of celery."

Roma Pollock Turnbow—Uniontown

1 lg. stalk CELERY, diced	1 can (8 oz.) sliced WATER
2 cans (10.75 oz. ea.) CREAM	CHESTNUTS
OF CHICKEN SOUP	1 1/2 cups BREAD CRUMBS
1/2 cup SUGAR	1/2 stick BUTTER
2 Tbsp. chopped PIMENTOS	1/2 cup slivered ALMONDS

In a saucepan, cover celery with water. Add salt and boil for 8 minutes; drain. In a bowl, mix together celery, soup, sugar, pimentos and water chestnuts. Pour mixture into a 2-quart casserole dish. Bake, covered, at 350° for 45 minutes. In a skillet, sauté bread crumbs in butter; stir in almonds. Remove casserole from oven and spread bread crumbs on top of celery mixture. Return to oven and bake for an additional 15 minutes. Serve hot.

Creamy Cheesy Potatoes

"I collect recipes and this one turned out to be a favorite! It is quite old and I still use it often."

Evelyn Ball—Ottawa

1 can (10.75 oz.) CREAM OF CHICKEN SOUP
3 cups shredded CHEDDAR CHEESE, divided
1 cup SOUR CREAM
3 GREEN ONIONS, chopped
SALT and PEPPER
8 POTATOES, peeled and thinly sliced

In a bowl, combine soup, 1 1/2 cups of cheese, sour cream and onions. Season with salt and pepper to taste and mix well. Stir in potatoes. Pour mixture into a greased 13 x 9 baking dish; sprinkle top with remaining cheese. Bake, uncovered, at 350° for 30-35 minutes or until potatoes are tender.

Serves 8-10.

Baked Stuffed Tomatoes

"I created my own version of this recipe after growing tired of the usual ingredients of mozzarella cheese and basil."

Patricia Polley—Columbus

3 slices BACON
4 lg. TOMATOES
3/4 cup shredded SHARP CHEDDAR CHEESE
1/2 cup DRY BREAD CRUMBS, plain or seasoned
1/4 cup finely diced ONION
2 Tbsp. finely diced GREEN BELL PEPPER

In a skillet, fry bacon until crisp; cool, drain on paper towels and then crumble. Cut a thin slice from the top of each tomato. Scoop out pulp and seeds; set aside for other use. In a bowl, combine bacon with remaining ingredients and mix well. Arrange tomatoes in a greased baking dish and fill each with the stuffing mixture. Bake at 375° for 25 minutes.

Did You Know?
On July 20, 1969, Neil Armstrong of Wapakoneta became the first man to walk on the moon!

Marinated Carrots

"This recipe came from a dear friend and is one of my favorites!"

Shirley Baston—The Blue Pencil, Fremont

2 lbs. CARROTS, cut into 1-inch pieces
1 lg. GREEN BELL PEPPER, cut into bite-size pieces
1 cup SUGAR
1 tsp. PEPPER
1/2 cup VINEGAR
1/4 cup WATER
1 lg. ONION, cut into bite-size pieces
1 can (10.75 oz.) CREAM OF TOMATO SOUP

In a saucepan, cook carrots in salted water until tender-crisp; drain. Combine remaining ingredients and add to carrots. Heat mixture and simmer until carrots are thoroughly heated. Delicious served hot or cold.

Old-Fashioned Cabbage Relish

"My Aunt Pauline remembers cutting the cabbage for this recipe for her mother, Grandma Sands. It's perfect with pork!"
Donna Sorrell—Amish Country Log Cabin Bed & Breakfast,
Winchester

1 head CABBAGE	6 cups SUGAR
10 GREEN TOMATOES	1 Tbsp. CELERY SEED
12 GREEN BELL PEPPERS	2 Tbsp. MUSTARD SEED
6 RED BELL PEPPERS	1 1/2 tsp. TURMERIC
4 cups chopped ONION	4 cups CIDER VINEGAR
1/2 cup SALT	2 cups WATER

Coarsely chop cabbage, tomatoes and bell peppers. Place in a large bowl, add onion and sprinkle with salt; let stand overnight. Rinse vegetables with water to remove all salt; drain. In a large saucepan, combine sugar, celery seed, mustard seed, turmeric, vinegar and water. Bring mixture to a boil, reduce heat and simmer for 3 minutes. Place vegetables in hot, sterilized pint jars. Pour liquid over vegetables to fill jars; seal with canning lids.

Makes 8 pints.

Broccoli-Dressing Delight
Roma Pollock Turnbow—Uniontown

1 pkg. (6 oz.) STOVE TOP® STUFFING
1 pkg. (16 oz.) frozen BROCCOLI PIECES
1 can (10.75 oz.) CREAM of CHICKEN SOUP
1/4 cup MILK
1 cup shredded CHEDDAR CHEESE
PAPRIKA

Prepare stuffing mix and cook broccoli according to package directions. Drain broccoli well. In a bowl, blend soup and milk together. Line a greased 13 x 9 baking dish with stuffing, pressing into bottom and up the sides. Arrange broccoli on stuffing and pour soup mixture over all. Sprinkle with cheese and garnish with paprika. Bake, uncovered, at 350° for 25 minutes.

Cheesy Zucchini

"I needed a new way to use an abundance of zucchini. This is easy to make and delicious."

Marilyn Frederick—Bellevue

4 cups diced ZUCCHINI (leave some peel for color)
3 EGGS, slightly beaten
1 cup MILK
1/4 cup MARGARINE or BUTTER, melted
1 jar (4 oz.) PIMENTOS, drained and chopped
1 1/2 cups crushed CHEESE CRACKERS or SALTINES
2 cups shredded SHARP CHEDDAR CHEESE
PAPRIKA

In a saucepan, cook zucchini in boiling salted water for 5 minutes; drain. In a bowl, combine remaining ingredients except for paprika. Add zucchini and mix well. Pour mixture into an 11 x 7 baking dish; sprinkle with paprika. Bake at 300° for 25-30 minutes until browned and bubbling.

Ohio Senator in Outer Space!

In 1962, John Glenn became the first American to orbit the earth. In 1998 at age 77, then-Senator Glenn became the oldest man to venture into outer space.

Smothered Cauliflower

"This is an attractive and delicious side dish."

Ruth Putman—Van Wert

1 head CAULIFLOWER
1/2 cup SOUR CREAM
1/2 cup MAYONNAISE
1 tsp. MUSTARD

3 GREEN ONIONS, chopped
1 cup grated CHEDDAR CHEESE

Trim leaves and stalk from cauliflower, leaving the head whole. Rinse cauliflower, cover with plastic wrap and place in a microwaveable bowl. Microwave on High for 10-15 minutes; drain. In another bowl, combine sour cream, mayonnaise, mustard, onions and cheese. Spread cheese mixture over cauliflower. Microwave for 1-2 minutes or until cheese is melted. Serve warm.

Corn & Zucchini Pudding

"This wonderful dish goes well with almost any meat. It's good year-around, but I especially like to include it in our Thanksgiving dinner menu."

Barbara Bratel Collier, *Food Editor*—Sun Newspapers, Cleveland

1 can (15 oz.) CREAM-STYLE CORN
1 can (15.25 oz.) WHOLE KERNEL CORN drained
    (or 2 cups fresh)
4 Tbsp. BUTTER or MARGARINE
1/2 cup chopped ONION
4 sm. unpared ZUCCHINI, cut into 1/4-inch thick rounds
GARLIC POWDER
2 EGGS beaten
1 cup MILK or 1/2 cup MILK and 1/2 cup HEAVY CREAM
SALT and freshly ground BLACK PEPPER
1/8 tsp. freshly grated NUTMEG
1 cup grated CHEDDAR CHEESE
1/3 cup grated PARMESAN CHEESE

Preheat oven to 375°. Combine both kinds of corn together in a bowl. In a skillet, melt butter; add onion and sauté until translucent. Stir in zucchini and corn mixture and cook until corn is slightly tender. Sprinkle with garlic powder to taste. Remove skillet from heat; blend in eggs, milk, salt, pepper and nutmeg. Add cheddar and Parmesan cheese and stir well. Pour mixture into a 5-cup baking dish. Bake for about 30 minutes or until set in center and top edges are golden.

Serves 6-8.

Cleveland

Cleveland, the largest city in Ohio, is one of the leading industrial centers of the United States. Its position on the shores of Lake Erie and at the mouth of the Cuyahoga River as well as the huge supplies of coal and iron ore nearby, helped make Cleveland an important steel producer. The Terminal Tower Building, one of the tallest buildings in the United States, rises 768 feet in Monumental Park in the downtown area.

Fresh Tomato Pie

"This is a delicious way to use up an abundance of fresh tomatoes, the official 'fruit' of Ohio."

Wilma Jagodnik—Richmond Heights

1 (9-inch) unbaked PIE SHELL
1 1/2 cups shredded MOZZARELLA CHEESE
4 sm. TOMATOES
1/2 cup loosely packed fresh BASIL LEAVES, chopped
2 lg. cloves GARLIC, finely minced
1/3 cup grated PARMESAN or ROMANO CHEESE
1/2 cup MAYONNAISE
WHITE PEPPER
Fresh BASIL LEAVES for garnish

Bake pie shell at 450° for 7-8 minutes and remove from oven; reduce oven temperature to 350°. Sprinkle 1/2 cup of mozzarella cheese onto hot crust; cool on wire rack. Cut tomatoes into thick slices or wedges and drain well on paper towels. Arrange tomatoes on top of cheese in crust. In a bowl, combine basil, garlic, Parmesan cheese, mayonnaise and pepper; mix well. Spread mixture over tomatoes; spread remaining mozzarella cheese on top Bake for 25-30 minutes or until cheese is melted and golden brown. Cool slightly before cutting. Garnish with basil leaves.

Helen's Scalloped Pineapple

"This is my cousin Helen's specialty dish, it's great with ham!."

Evelyn Ball—Ottawa

3 EGGS, beaten
3/4 cup SUGAR
1/2 cup MILK
1/3 cup MARGARINE, melted
1 can (15.25 oz.) CRUSHED PINEAPPLE, drained
8 slices BREAD, cut into small pieces

In a bowl, mix all ingredients together. Spoon into a greased casserole dish. Bake at 450° for 10 minutes; reduce oven temperature to 350° and bake for an additional 30 minutes.

Breads

Date Nut Bread

*"My grandmother baked this bread every Christmas. Now I
carry on her tradition, using her old, solid tin cans."*

Gail Heffner-Charles—Pataskala

2 tsp. BAKING SODA	2 EGGS, beaten
1 lb. pitted DATES, cut into	2 tsp. VANILLA
small pieces	1 tsp. SALT
2 cups BOILING WATER	4 cups FLOUR, sifted
2 cups SUGAR	1 1/4 cups chopped
1/2 cup CRISCO®	ENGLISH WALNUTS

In a small bowl, sprinkle baking soda over dates. Add
boiling water, stir well and set aside. In another bowl, cream
together sugar and Crisco. Add eggs, vanilla and salt. Stir in
flour alternately with date mixture and mix well. Fold in nuts.
Grease and flour the insides of 6 (19-ounce) tin cans. Fill each
can 1/2 full with batter. Bake at 325° for 1 hour. Allow bread
to cool; remove from cans. Cut into 1/2-inch slices and serve
plain or spread with cream cheese and top with parsley, sliced
pimentos, stuffed olives or grated cheese.

Marble "Kuchen"

"Tom's grandmother used to make this all the time and the great-grandchildren loved it so much. After she passed away, Tom took over baking this dish and everyone still loves it!"

Tom and Kathy Fordos—Mirabelle Bed & Breakfast, Wooster

1 cup MARGARINE	2 tsp. BAKING POWDER
4 EGGS	4 1/3 cups FLOUR
1 1/3 cups SUGAR	1 1/2 cups MILK
1/2 tsp. VANILLA	3 heaping tsp. NESTLE'S QUICK®
1/2 tsp. LEMON EXTRACT	or POWDERED COCOA

Preheat oven to 430°. In a mixing bowl, blend margarine, eggs, sugar, vanilla and lemon extract until smooth and creamy. Sift baking powder and flour together. Add 3 cups flour mixture to egg mixture, one cup at a time, until well-blended. Slowly mix in 1/2 cup milk and continue blending. Add remaining flour and beat until creamy. Add 1/2 cup milk, blend, then add remaining milk, blending until batter is smooth. Grease and flour 2 loaf pans. Pour 1/3 of batter into each loaf pan. In remaining 1/3 of batter, mix in Nestle's Quick. Divide and pour mixture on top of batter in each loaf pan. With a large spoon, swirl or stir slightly to achieve a marbled effect when baked. Reduce heat to 410° and bake for 60 minutes or until toothpick inserted into center comes out clean. Cool for 10 minutes, then remove from pans and cool on wire racks.

Makes 2 loaves.

Dayton

Settlers from Cincinnati founded this city in 1796 because of the three rivers—the Mad, the Miami and the Stillwater—that flow together here, making it a natural center of water transportation. Dayton is called the "Birthplace of Aviation" because Orville and Wilbur Wright, who invented the first successful airplane, lived here. The U.S. Air Force Museum at nearby Wright-Patterson Air Force Base is a favorite tourist destination.

Butter Brickle Bread

"I cherish this recipe given to me by a long-time friend."

Evelyn Ball—Ottawa

1 pkg. (18 oz.) BUTTER
   PECAN CAKE MIX
1 pkg. (3 oz.) INSTANT COCONUT
   PUDDING MIX
1/4 cup OIL

4 EGGS
1 cup HOT WATER
1 tsp. VANILLA
1 cup chopped NUTS,
   (optional)

In a mixing bowl, combine all ingredients and beat at high speed for 2 minutes. Pour into 3 greased and floured loaf pans. Bake at 350° for 15 minutes. Reduce heat to 300° and bake for an additional 45 minutes.

Did You Know?

Moses Cleaveland, a surveyor for the Connecticut Land Company, founded Cleveland in 1796. The village was named after Cleaveland, but a newspaper printer misspelled the name in 1831 and it has been known as Cleveland ever since!

Corn Pone

In Indian tradition, this same basic cornbread (called ashcake) was baked in the hot ashes of an open fire. Later it was baked in the fire on a hoe and called hoecake. Today it is known as corn pone or journey (Johnny) cake.

2 cups WHITE CORNMEAL
1 tsp. SALT
1/4 tsp. BAKING SODA

4 Tbsp. SHORTENING
3/4 cup BOILING WATER
1/2 cup BUTTERMILK

Sift together cornmeal, salt and baking soda. Work in shortening with finger tips until well-blended. Pour in boiling water and continue to work the mixture. Gradually add enough buttermilk to make a soft dough, but one firm enough to be molded or patted into small, flat cakes. Place cakes in a hot, well-greased iron skillet and bake 35-40 minutes in a 350° oven.

Makes 12 cakes.

Banana-Oatmeal Muffins

"For the last ten years I have featured these muffins at our Bed & Breakfast. I developed the recipe from one that my sister gave me. The guest books in each of the rooms have glowing comments about it."

Jo Ellen Cuthbertson—The Red Gables Bed & Breakfast,
Sandusky

1 cup FLOUR
1 1/4 cups OATS
3 tsp. BAKING POWDER
1/2 tsp. SALT
1/4 tsp. CINNAMON
1/3 cup OIL

1/2 cup SUGAR
1/2 cup packed BROWN
   SUGAR
2 EGGS
2 BANANAS, mashed

In a bowl, combine flour, oats, baking powder, salt and cinnamon; mix well. In another bowl, combine oil, sugar, brown sugar, eggs and bananas; mix well. Combine mixtures and stir well. Pour into generously greased muffin tins. Bake at 400° for 20 minutes.

Makes 12 muffins.

Poppy Seed Bread

"This is one of those recipes that you have been making for so long you don't remember where you got it!"

Shirley Baston—The Blue Pencil, Fremont

3/4 cup OIL
1 1/2 cups SUGAR
2 EGGS, beaten
1 cup MILK
2 cups FLOUR
1 Tbsp. POPPY SEEDS

1 tsp. VANILLA
1 tsp. BUTTER FLAVORING
1 tsp. ALMOND FLAVORING
1/4 tsp. PEPPER
1 tsp. SALT

Combine all ingredients in a bowl and mix for 2 minutes. Pour into 2 greased and floured loaf pans. Bake at 350° for 1 hour and 15 minutes. Allow to cool for 10 minutes, then remove from pans.

Makes 2 loaves.

Apple-Pumpkin Streusel Muffins

"Apples are a primary fall crop in Ohio. One of the country's largest Pumpkin Festivals is held annually in Circleville just south of Columbus. About 15 years ago, I created this recipe with my niece who visited on weekends and loved to bake."

Patricia Polley—Columbus

2 1/2 cups FLOUR
1 cup SUGAR
1 tsp. CINNAMON
1 tsp. NUTMEG
1/2 tsp. ALLSPICE
1/2 tsp. SALT
1 cup canned PUMPKIN

1/2 cup VEGETABLE OIL
2 EGGS, slightly beaten
1 tsp. VANILLA
1/2 cup chopped PECANS
1 3/4 cups peeled and finely
    chopped APPLES

Streusel Filling:
    1/2 cup packed DARK BROWN
        SUGAR
    2 tsp. CINNAMON
    1/2 cup finely chopped PECANS
    2 Tbsp. BUTTER, melted

In a bowl, combine flour, sugar and spices. In another bowl, combine pumpkin, oil, eggs, vanilla and pecans and mix well. Add pumpkin mixture to dry ingredients and stir until moistened. Fold in apples. Spoon into greased muffin tins, filling each cup 1/3 full. To make streusel filling: In a small bowl, combine filling ingredients and stir. Sprinkle filling evenly over each muffin cup, then top with remaining batter, filling cups 3/4 full. Bake at 350° for 35-40 minutes or until toothpick inserted in center comes out clean.

Makes 8 large muffins.

Ohio's State Capitals

Chillicothe was the first capital of Ohio (1803 to 1810). Zanesville became the capital in 1810 and then Chillicothe was again the capital in 1812. Columbus became the permanent capital in 1816.

Mom's
Pineapple-Nut Bread

"I won first place with this recipe at the Scioto County Fair."

Phyllis A. Price—Lucasville

3 cups FLOUR
2 cups SUGAR
1 tsp. BAKING SODA
1 tsp. CINNAMON
3 lg. EGGS, beaten
1 can (20 oz.) CRUSHED
  PINEAPPLE, drained

1 cup VEGETABLE OIL
1 tsp. VANILLA
1 cup chopped PECANS or
  WALNUTS
2 cups mashed BANANAS
  or chopped APPLES

Preheat oven to 350°. In a bowl, combine all dry ingredients. Make a "well" in center of dry ingredients and add remaining ingredients. Stir gently until just moistened. Pour into a greased and floured Bundt pan or 2 loaf pans. Bake for 1 hour or until toothpick inserted in center comes out clean.

Yeast Rolls

"My friend, Donna Deemer, gave me this recipe. These are the best rolls, very light and good. The longer the dough is refrigerated, the better the rolls are."

Frances L. Wright—Portsmouth

1 pkg. (1 oz.) dry YEAST
2 cups WARM WATER
1 Tbsp. SALT
8 Tbsp. SUGAR

3 Tbsp. CRISCO® OIL
2 EGGS, slightly beaten
6-8 cups FLOUR

Dissolve yeast in 2 cups warm water. In a large bowl, mix together salt, sugar and oil. Add eggs, stir in yeast and mix well. Add flour until dough is soft and kneadable. Turn dough out onto a floured surface and knead; place in a greased bowl. Cover and let rise for 1 1/2 hours. Punch dough down and refrigerate. When ready to make rolls, place equal portions (clover-leaf style) in greased muffin tins and allow to rise. Bake in a preheated oven at 400° for 15-20 minutes. Brush tops with butter after removing from oven.

Bran Muffins

"This was one of my mother's favorite recipes. Both of my children now make these for their families."

Billi Schmidt—Dayton

1/2 cup OATS
1 cup ALL-BRAN® CEREAL
1 can (8 oz.) crushed PINEAPPLE,
 drained, juice reserved
1 EGG, beaten
3/4 cup SUGAR
1 tsp. SALT

1/4 cup OIL
1 cup BUTTERMILK
1 1/2 tsp. BAKING SODA
1 1/2 cups FLOUR
1 cup coarsely chopped
 WALNUTS

Glaze:
 1 Tbsp. reserved PINEAPPLE JUICE
 1/2 cup POWDERED SUGAR

In a bowl, combine oats and cereal. In a small saucepan, place 1/2 cup of reserved pineapple juice and bring it to a boil; pour over cereal mixture and allow to cool. Stir in egg and remaining ingredients until well-blended. Grease muffin cups and fill 3/4 full with batter. Bake at 400° for 15 minutes. Cool slightly and remove from muffin pans. To prepare glaze: In a small bowl, combine remaining pineapple juice* and powdered sugar; stir until smooth. Spoon glaze over baked muffins.

*Orange juice can be used if there is not enough pineapple juice.

Makes 18-20 muffins.

Toledo

This city ranks as the largest producer of automotive parts in the United States and is called the "Glass Capital of the World" because four of the nation's largest glass-manufacturing companies are headquartered here. The city ranks as one of the world's leading shippers of coal and serves as a trading center for the rich agricultural region in northwestern Ohio. Toledo, a major Great Lakes port, is an important water gateway to the western United States.

Orange Scones with American Clotted Cream

"In 1995 I opened a tea room in our home. Afternoon tea was popular with Ohio's Victorian ladies and I find that people enjoy returning to that gentle time by 'taking tea'."

Nancy Stahl—Victorian Afternoon Teas, Bryan

2 cups FLOUR
1/3 cup SUGAR
2 1/2 tsp. BAKING POWDER
Pinch of SALT
3 Tbsp. BUTTER, chilled and cut
    into small pieces
1 ctn. (8 oz.) LEMON or VANILLA
    YOGURT
1/4 cup ORANGE JUICE
1 Tbsp. grated DRY ORANGE PEEL
1 Tbsp. SUGAR

Combine first 4 ingredients in a mixing bowl and cut in butter until mixture resembles a coarse meal. Add yogurt, orange juice and orange peel and stir just until moistened; dough will be sticky. With floured hands, place dough on a greased baking sheet and pat into a 9-inch circle. Score dough into 10 wedges and sprinkle with sugar. Bake at 400° for 15 minutes or until golden brown. Serve with ***American Clotted Cream*** and your favorite jam or jelly.

American Clotted Cream

"The English use unpasturized milk to make toppings for scones. I use pasturized products for mine."

1 pkg. (8 oz.) CREAM CHEESE, softened
3 Tbsp. SUGAR
1/2 cup WHIPPING CREAM
1 tsp. VANILLA

In a bowl, whip cream cheese, then add sugar and whipping cream. Beat in vanilla. Continue beating until semi-thick and smooth. Cover and refrigerate until ready to serve.

Desserts

Cherry Filled
White Chocolate Squares

*"My recipe won 1st Place in 1998 at the Wayne County Fair
4-H Bake Off when I was 13 years old!"*

Lori Arnold—Orrville

1/2 cup BUTTER	1/2 tsp. SALT
2 cups VANILLA CHIPS	1/2 tsp. ALMOND EXTRACT
2 EGGS	1/2 cup CHERRY JAM
1/2 cup SUGAR	1/2 cup shredded COCONUT
1 cup FLOUR	1/4 cup sliced ALMONDS

In a small saucepan, melt butter over low heat. Remove
from heat and add 1 cup of vanilla chips; do not stir. In a mixing
bowl, beat eggs and gradually add sugar until blended; stir in
vanilla chip mixture. Add flour, salt and extract and stir well.
Spread 1/2 of the batter in a greased and floured 8 x 8 baking
pan. Bake at 325 ° for 20 minutes. In a small saucepan, melt
jam over low heat, then spread evenly over baked mixture. Top
with remaining batter, vanilla chips, coconut and almonds.
Bake at 325° for 20-25 minutes or until light brown. Allow to
cool before cutting into squares.

Grandma Burns' Zucchini Pie

"Thirty years ago our little garden in southern Ohio was running over with zucchini. I prepared zucchini every way: I fried it, pickled it and added it to cupcakes, cookies and breads. Zucchini actually turned out to be our favorite vegetable!"

Evelyn Johnson Burns—Portsmouth

4 cups peeled, sliced ZUCCHINI, seeds removed	1 tsp. CINNAMON
	1 tsp. CREAM OF TARTAR
1 cup packed BROWN SUGAR	1 (9-inch) unbaked PIE
1 cup WARM WATER	SHELL
1/2 cup SUGAR	

Cook zucchini in salted water until tender; drain well. Place zucchini in a medium bowl, add warm water, white and brown sugars, cinnamon and cream of tartar and mix well. Pour into pie shell. Bake at 350° until golden brown or set. Remove from oven and allow to cool.

Zanesville

This city was named after Ebenezer Zane who settled here in 1797. His great-grandson, Zane Grey, became a well-known novelist. Once considered the pottery capital of the United States, many pottery factories are still in operation here.

Cranberry Crunch

Rosie Sutter—Ottawa

1 can (16 oz.) WHOLE CRANBERRY SAUCE	1/4 cup ALL-PURPOSE FLOUR
	4 Tbsp. BUTTER
1/2 cup QUICK-COOKING OATS	WHIPPED CREAM or
1/2 cup packed BROWN SUGAR	VANILLA ICE CREAM

Preheat oven to 350°. Spread cranberry sauce in the bottom of a 9-inch pie pan. In a small bowl, combine oats, brown sugar and flour; cut in butter until mixture is crumbly. Sprinkle mixture over cranberry sauce. Bake for 25 minutes. When serving, top with whipped cream or ice cream.

Helen's Bread Pudding with Lemon Sauce

"This is our great-great aunt Helen Hess' recipe."

Lakalynn Arnold—Orrville

6 slices DAY-OLD WHITE
   BREAD
2 Tbsp. BUTTER or
   MARGARINE, melted
1 1/2 cups + 2 Tbsp. SUGAR
1 tsp. CINNAMON

1/2 cup RAISINS
4 EGGS
Dash of SALT
2 cups MILK
2 tsp. VANILLA

Preheat oven to 350°. Brush bread slices with butter. In a small bowl, mix 2 tablespoons sugar and cinnamon together and sprinkle on bread. Cut each slice into quarters. Arrange layers of bread and raisins in a greased 1 1/2-quart baking dish. In a medium bowl, beat eggs, then stir in remaining sugar, salt, milk and vanilla; continue to stir until sugar is dissolved. Pour over bread and raisins. Place baking dish in the center of a larger baking pan filled with 1 inch of hot water. Bake for 55-60 minutes or until knife inserted 1/2-inch from the edge comes out clean. Serve pudding warm or chilled, with ***Lemon Sauce.***

Lemon Sauce

1/2 cup BUTTER
1 cup SUGAR
1 EGG, beaten

1/2 cup BOILING WATER
Juice and grated rind
   of 1 LEMON

In a small bowl, cream butter and sugar together. Stir in egg, water, lemon juice and lemon rind. Pour into top half of double boiler, add water to bottom half and cook sauce until thickened.

Steamboats in Lake Erie

In 1818, the steamboat "Walk-in-the-Water" became the first steamboat on Lake Erie, demonstrating the pactical use of the Great Lakes as a waterway to the West. The Erie Canal, the Ohio and Erie Canal and the Miami and Erie Canals served as busy trade routes for more than 25 years.

Fresh Raspberry Pie

"We used to pick wild raspberries and my mom would can 100 quarts a season. After her canning was done, she would make jelly and delicious berry pies."

Phyllis A. Price—Lucasville

Pie Crust:
    2 cups FLOUR
    2/3 cup SHORTENING
    6 Tbsp. COLD WATER

Pie Filling:
    1 qt. WILD RASPBERRIES
    1 1/4 cups SUGAR
    2 Tbsp. FLOUR

1 Tbsp. SUGAR
1/4 tsp. CINNAMON

Preheat oven to 350°. In a medium bowl, blend flour and shortening together. Add water a little at a time and mix until dough is soft; divide into 2 parts. Turn dough out onto a floured surface and roll out into 1/4-inch thick circles. Place 1 crust in a 9-inch pie pan. Place raspberries in a bowl. In another bowl, mix sugar and flour together and then gently stir into the raspberries; spoon into pie crust. Cover with top crust and flute edges to seal; cut small slits in top crust. Combine sugar and cinnamon and sprinkle on top of pie. Bake for 1 hour until crust is golden brown.

Youngstown's Mill Creek Park

Youngstown is the home of Mill Creek Park, one of the nation's most beautiful natural parks. This 2,500-acre park contains three lakes, a 6-mile-long gorge, Lanterman Falls and the 12-acre Fellows Riverside Gardens that displays more than 30,000 tulips that bloom each spring. You can test your golfing skills at two golf courses (designed by Donald Ross) that are within the park.

Buckeyes

"Since our state tree is the Buckeye, these Buckeye candies are a true representation of Ohio."

Sharon Partezana—East Liverpool

1 1/2 cups POWDERED SUGAR
1 1/4 cups PEANUT BUTTER (smooth or crunchy)
4 Tbsp. BUTTER, softened
1 pkg. (6 oz.) CHOCOLATE CHIPS
1 tsp. SHORTENING

In a medium bowl, mix powdered sugar, peanut butter and butter until well-blended, kneading with hands if necessary. Shape mixture into 1-inch balls and place in a single layer in a jelly roll pan. Cover and refrigerate for 2 hours or until firm. Melt chocolate chips and shortening in a double boiler. Dip peanut butter balls into the chocolate or pour the chocolate over them, leaving a small circle uncovered, for the "buckeye look."

Johnny Appleseed Cake

"While traveling through Ohio, Johnny Appleseed planted apple trees near the Defiance Trail northeast of Spencerville. This delicious cake is made in his honor."

Claire Morgret—Elida

1 pkg. (18.25 oz.) YELLOW CAKE MIX
1 can (21 oz.) APPLE PIE FILLING
3 EGGS
3 Tbsp. SUGAR
1 tsp. CINNAMON

In a large bowl, combine cake mix, pie filling and eggs; beat 2 minutes at medium speed. Mix sugar and cinnamon together in a small bowl. Spread 1/2 of the batter in a greased 13 x 9 pan; sprinkle 1/2 of the sugar/cinnamon mixture on top. Lightly spread remaining batter on top; sprinkle with remaining sugar/cinnamon mixture. Bake at 350° for 30-35 minutes or until a toothpick inserted in the center comes out clean. Serve warm with a scoop of vanilla ice cream, if desired.

Mom's Butterscotch Pie

"This is a recipe my mother gave to me. I like it because it is so easy to make and delicious too!"

Katherine C. Bradshaw—Elida

1 cup packed LIGHT BROWN
    SUGAR
3 Tbsp. FLOUR
2 EGGS, separated
1 cup WARM WATER

1/2 stick MARGARINE
1 tsp. VANILLA
1 (9-inch) baked PIE SHELL
1/4 cup SUGAR

In a bowl, combine brown sugar with flour; add egg yolks and blend. Gradually stir in warm water and mix until smooth. Pour in a saucepan and cook over medium to low heat. Add margarine; stir until thickened, then add vanilla. Pour mixture into pie shell; allow to cool slightly. In a small mixing bowl, beat egg whites until soft peaks form. Gradually add sugar and beat until egg whites are shiny and stiff peaks form. Spread on top of pie filling to the edge of crust. Bake at 350° until top is golden brown.

Chocolate Mint Angel Cake

"Since we are in the herb capital of Ohio, I think this is a good representation. The chocolate mint geranium leaf is used here."

Jama L. Cumbo—Gahanna Historical Society Inc.,Gahanna

1 box (16.75 oz.) ANGEL FOOD CAKE MIX
2 Tbsp. GREEN CRÈME DE MENTHE
1/2 cup MINIATURE CHOCOLATE CHIPS
4-6 CHOCOLATE MINT LEAVES

In a small bowl, prepare egg whites according to package directions, replacing 2 tablespoons water with crème de menthe. In a large bowl, prepare cake mix; fold in egg white mixture. Gently fold in chocolate chips. Place chocolate mint leaves upside down in the bottom of an angel food cake pan. Pour batter over leaves. Bake according to directions.

Cranberry Cake with Caramel Sauce

Ellen Grinsfelder—Inn at Cedar Falls, Logan

2 cups ALL-PURPOSE FLOUR
1/2 cup SUGAR
2 tsp. BAKING POWDER
1 1/2 Tbsp. BUTTER
1 cup MILK
3 cups fresh CRANBERRIES, halved

In a bowl, sift together flour, sugar and baking powder. Cut in butter until mixture resembles meal; stir in milk and cranberries. Line the bottom of a buttered 9-inch round cake pan with waxed paper; butter and flour the waxed paper. Pour batter into pan. Bake at 350° for 45 minutes or until sides pull slightly away from pan. Allow cake to cool in the pan for 30 minutes, then place on wire rack. Remove waxed paper and cool completely. Serve cake with warm *Caramel Sauce.*

Caramel Sauce

1/2 cup packed BROWN SUGAR   1/2 cup HEAVY CREAM
1/2 cup SUGAR   2 Tbsp. BUTTER

In a saucepan, combine sugars, cream and butter. Bring mixture to a boil over moderate heat, stirring constantly until sugar is dissolved.

Put-in-Bay on South Bass Island

This village (population approximately 450), boasts caves, wineries and fish hatcheries. It is also the site of Perry's Victory and International Peace Memorial. The 352-foot-high memorial is built of pink granite and has an observation deck at the top. The memorial commemorates Commodore Oliver Perry's defeat of a British fleet that had been controlling Lake Erie. His famous message to General Harrison: "We have met the enemy and they are ours."

Chocolate-Raspberry Truffle Tart

"This is a delicious dessert– cool and not too sweet."
Anne Jagodnik—Richmond Heights

25 CHOCOLATE WAFER COOKIES, crushed
5 Tbsp. UNSALTED BUTTER, softened
3/4 cup SEEDLESS RASPBERRY JAM
8 sq. (1 oz. ea.) SEMI-SWEET CHOCOLATE, chopped
1 cup HEAVY CREAM
2 cups fresh RASPBERRIES

Combine cookie crumbs with butter and press mixture on the bottom and up the sides of a 9-inch tart pan (with removable bottom). In a saucepan, heat jam just until melted; spread evenly over crust. Freeze for 10-15 minutes to set. In another saucepan, combine chocolate and cream. Cook over low heat, stirring constantly until chocolate is melted and mixture is smooth. Pour over jam and refrigerate for 3-4 hours or until chocolate is set. When ready to serve, remove tart from pan, place on serving platter and arrange raspberries on top.

Serves 10-12.

Bread Pudding

"When I was growing up nothing went to waste. Mom made this pudding for us when a loaf of bread got too dry for regular use."
Darlene Poehler—Nicollet

2 EGGS, slightly beaten
2 1/2 cups MILK
1/2 cup SUGAR
1 tsp. VANILLA
1/4 tsp. SALT

1 tsp. CINNAMON
5 slices stale BREAD, torn into pieces
1/3 cup RAISINS
Dash of NUTMEG

In a large mixing bowl, combine eggs, milk, sugar, vanilla, salt and cinnamon and stir well; add bread and mix lightly. Gently stir in raisins and nutmeg. Pour into a greased 1 1/2-quart casserole dish. Bake at 350° for 45-50 minutes or until a knife inserted in the center comes out clean.

Upside Down Apple-Pecan Pie

"This recipe combines apples, which are plentiful in the southern Ohio orchards, and the great taste of pecans."

Marianne Lucas—West Portsmouth

1 cup chopped PECANS	2 Tbsp. FLOUR
1/2 cup packed BROWN SUGAR	1/2 tsp. CINNAMON
	1/8 tsp. NUTMEG
1/3 cup BUTTER, melted	6 med. GOLDEN DELICIOUS
2 (9-inch) unbaked PIE CRUSTS	APPLES, peeled, sliced
1/4 cup SUGAR	thin

Preheat oven to 375°. In a 9-inch pie plate, combine pecans, brown sugar and butter; spread evenly over bottom of pan. Place bottom pie crust over pecan mixture in pan. In a large bowl, combine apples, sugar, flour, cinnamon and nutmeg and mix lightly. Spoon mixture into pie crust. Top with the second pie crust and flute edges; cut several slits in top. Place pan on foil or cookie sheet during baking to safeguard against spillage. Bake for 40-50 minutes or until crust is golden brown and apples are tender. Cool pie upright in pan for 5 minutes then place a serving plate over the pie, invert and carefully remove the pan. Cool at least 1 hour before serving.

Ohio's Apples

Fall is the perfect time to try the many varieties of Ohio apples. Select firm apples, free of bruises, decay, broken or shriveled skin. Fruit should be ripe when picked to have good flavor, texture and storing ability. Refrigerate apples in a perforated, plastic bag at 32-35°. Ohio's apple varieties include: Summer, McIntosh, Jonathon, Red Delicious, Golden Delicious, Law Rome, Stayman, Empire and Melrose. Ohio specialty apples include: Crispin, Criterion, Fuji, Gala, Granny Smith and Red Cort.

Chocolate Drizzle Cream Cheese Roll-Ups

"This recipe has become a favorite of our guests."

Pat Borton—Cornerstone Inn B & B, Archbold

1/2 cup POWDERED SUGAR
1 pkg. (8 oz.) CREAM CHEESE, softened
3 tsp. KAHLÚA® LIQUEUR
1 tsp. VANILLA
1/2 cup finely chopped PECANS
2 cans (8 oz. ea.) CRESCENT ROLLS

Glaze:
  1/2 cup CHOCOLATE CHIPS
  1 tsp. CRISCO®

Preheat oven to 350°. In a bowl, combine powdered sugar, cream cheese, Kahlúa and vanilla and blend well; stir in pecans. Separate crescent rolls into 12 triangles. Spoon 1 heaping tablespoon of cream cheese mixture onto the shortest side of each triangle. Roll up, starting at the shortest side. Place roll-up, point side down, on a greased cookie sheet. Bake for 12-15 minutes or until golden brown; allow to cool slightly. In a saucepan, heat chocolate chips and shortening over low heat; stir until chocolate is melted and mixture is smooth. Drizzle over warm roll-ups. Store in refrigerator.

Sorghum Cookies

"This is my grandmother's recipe from the early 1950s."

Ann Scohy—Dayton

1 cup SUGAR
2 EGGS, beaten
1 cup SORGHUM MOLASSES
1 tsp. VANILLA

4 cups FLOUR
1 tsp. SALT
1 tsp. BAKING SODA
1 tsp. CINNAMON

In a mixing bowl, combine all ingredients and mix well. Drop by heaping teaspoons onto a greased cookie sheet. Bake at 375° for 6-8 minutes.

Drumstick Dessert

Marilyn Ellerbrock—Glandorf Telephone Company Inc., Ottawa

2 cups GRAHAM CRACKER CRUMBS
1 stick MARGARINE, melted
2/3 cup chopped NUTS
1/3 cup + 1 1/2 Tbsp. PEANUT BUTTER, divided
1 pkg. (8 oz.) CREAM CHEESE, softened
1 cup POWDERED SUGAR
3 cups COOL WHIP®, divided
1 pkg. (3.5 oz.) INSTANT VANILLA PUDDING MIX
1 pkg. (3.9 oz.) INSTANT CHOCOLATE PUDDING MIX
2 cups COLD MILK
SHREDDED CHOCOLATE or CHOCOLATE CURLS for garnish

In a bowl, combine graham cracker crumbs with margarine, nuts and 1 1/2 tablespoons of peanut butter and blend well. Reserve 1/2 cup of graham cracker mixture. Press remaining mixture in bottom of a 13 x 9 baking pan. In a separate bowl, combine remaining peanut butter, cream cheese and powdered sugar; fold in 2 cups of Cool Whip and blend well. Spread mixture over crust. In a bowl, combine pudding mixes and milk and stir until pudding starts to set. Spread pudding over top of cream cheese mixture. Top with remaining Cool Whip and sprinkle with reserved graham cracker crumb mixture. Garnish with shredded chocolate or chocolate curls.

Ohio in Print and On the Air

The first newspaper published north and west of the Ohio River, the "Centinel of the North-Western Territory", was founded in Cincinnati in 1793. Ohio's oldest radio station, WHK, began broadcasting in Cleveland in 1922. In that same year, Ohio State University in Columbus started WOSU, the first educational radio station in North America. The first Ohio television station, WEWS-TV, opened in Cleveland in 1947.

Apple Dapple

"I have won many Apple Festival and County Fair baking contests with my apple cake, apple pie and apple butter recipes."

Esther McCoy—*Steubenville Herald-Star*, Steubenville

1/4 cup BUTTER
1 cup SUGAR
1 EGG
1 cup FLOUR
1 tsp. BAKING SODA

1/2 tsp. SALT
3/4 tsp. CINNAMON
1/2 tsp. NUTMEG
2 cups grated APPLE
1/2 cup chopped NUTS

Sauce:
1/2 cup BUTTER
1/2 cup CREAM

1 cup SUGAR

In a mixing bowl, cream together butter and sugar; add egg and beat well. In a separate bowl, sift together flour, baking soda, salt, cinnamon and nutmeg. Add flour mixture to creamed mixture; stir in apples and nuts. Pour into a buttered 8-inch baking pan. Bake at 350° for 45 minutes. To prepare sauce: In a saucepan, combine butter, cream and sugar. Bring mixture to a boil; reduce heat and simmer for 20 minutes, stirring constantly. Serve warm over cake squares.

Date Pudding

"A friend gave me this recipe. She has been making this pudding for over 50 years!"

Elizabeth Myers—Columbus

1 1/2 cups WATER
1 1/2 cups packed BROWN
   SUGAR
2 Tbsp. BUTTER
1/2 cup chopped DATES

1/2 cup MILK
1/4 cup chopped NUTS
1 cup FLOUR
2 tsp. BAKING POWDER\
1/2 tsp. SALT

In a saucepan, combine water with 1 cup brown sugar and 1 tablespoon butter. Boil for 3 minutes, then pour into a greased 2-quart casserole dish. Cream remaining butter and brown sugar together; stir in dates, milk, nuts, flour, baking powder and salt. Pour into the casserole dish. Bake at 300-350° until top is brown.

Apple-Raspberry Crumb Pie

This winning recipe by Esther McCoy of Dillonvale was published in the Ohio Apple Marketing Program recipe book.

Ohio Fruit & Vegetable Growers Association—Columbus

Crumb Topping:
- 1 cup FLOUR
- 1/2 cup packed BROWN SUGAR
- 1/2 tsp. CINNAMON
- 1/2 tsp. grated LEMON PEEL
- 6 Tbsp. BUTTER or MARGARINE
- 1/2 cup chopped WALNUTS or PECANS

Filling:
- 4-5 cups peeled and sliced APPLES (Jonathan, Melrose, Fuji or Paula Red)
- 1 1/2 cups fresh or frozen BLACK RASPBERRIES
- 3/4 cup SUGAR
- 4 Tbsp. FLOUR
- 3/4 tsp. CINNAMON
- 1/4 tsp. CLOVES

1 (9-inch) unbaked PIE SHELL

Preheat oven to 350°. To prepare crumb topping: In a mixing bowl, combine flour, brown sugar, cinnamon and lemon peel; cut in butter until mixture is crumbly. Add nuts and set aside. To prepare filling: In a bowl, combine fruits and sprinkle with sugar, flour, cinnamon and cloves. Pour into pie shell and cover with the crumb topping. Place pie on a cookie sheet and bake for 1 hour or until apples are tender.

Cleveland's
♫♪♫ Rock & Roll Hall of Fame & Museum

Exhibits chart the evolution of rock and roll, including everything from the blues to soul, punk to grunge. More than 150,000 square feet of exhibit space on seven floors capture the ever-evolving spirit of rock and roll. The Museum is truly a unique high-energy experience covering decades of music.

Apple Buckeyes

Emily Schirack—Canton

2 cups FLOUR	1/4 tsp. CINNAMON
1 tsp. SALT	1/4 tsp. NUTMEG
2 tsp. BAKING POWDER	1/4 cup APPLESAUCE
1 1/2 sticks BUTTER	1-2 Tbsp. WATER
1/2 cup MILK	1 APPLE, cut into 1-inch
1/2 cup SUGAR	pieces
2 Tbsp. BROWN SUGAR	2 Tbsp. APPLE JELLY

In a bowl, combine flour, salt and baking powder; cut in butter until mixture is crumbly. Stir in milk and mix into a soft dough. Place dough on a floured surface and roll out to 1/4-inch thickness. In a separate bowl, combine white and brown sugar, spices, applesauce and water; mixture should be thick. Stir in apple pieces until coated. Cut dough into squares large enough to hold apple pieces. Place one apple piece, with extra sauce, on dough square and fold up edges. Place on a greased baking sheet. Continue until all dough is used. In a saucepan, heat apple jelly until it melts; brush on unbaked "buckeyes"; sprinkle top with sugar. Bake at 350° for 25-35 minutes or until golden brown; allow to cool on baking sheet, then move to wire racks.

Popcorn Cake

Lisa Arnold—Orrville

1 bag (16 oz.) M & M'S®	1/4 cup VEGETABLE OIL
1/2 lb. COCKTAIL NUTS	1 bag (16 oz.) MINIATURE
4 qts. POPPED POPCORN	MARSHMALLOWS
1/4 cup MARGARINE or BUTTER	

In a mixing bowl, combine M & M's, nuts and popcorn. In a saucepan, combine margarine, oil and marshmallows. Cook over low heat until marshmallows have melted. Pour over popcorn mixture and mix well. Lightly press mixture into a well-greased Bundt pan, then invert onto a plate. Allow cake to stiffen before cutting.

Four-Stack Chocolate Pudding Dessert

"This is a special treat from Grandmother Ella."

Martha Clear—Dayton

First Stack:

1 stick MARGARINE, melted	1 Tbsp. SUGAR
1 cup FLOUR	1/2 cup finely chopped NUTS

In a bowl, combine margarine, flour, sugar and nuts. Spread mixture evenly in a 13 x 9 baking pan. Bake at 350° for 15 minutes; remove and allow to cool.

Second Stack:

1 pkg. (8 oz.) CREAM CHEESE, softened	2 cups COOL WHIP®
1 cup POWDERED SUGAR	

In a bowl, combine cream cheese and powdered sugar and blend well; fold in Cool Whip. Spread over crust.

Third Stack:

2 pkgs. (3.9 oz. ea.) INSTANT CHOCOLATE PUDDING MIX
3 cups COLD MILK

In a bowl, combine pudding mix with milk and stir until smooth. Spread over cream cheese mixture.

Fourth Stack:
COOL WHIP®

Top with Cool Whip. Chill and serve.

Sandusky

This city, on Sandusky Bay, a natural harbor on Lake Erie formed by the Cedar Point and Marblehead peninsulas, is one of the largest coal-shipping ports on the Great Lakes. Cedar Point, a 364-acre amusement/theme park and resort opened here in 1870. Visit too, the Merry-Go-Round Museum which features a working merry-go-round, animals and chariots from carousels, photographs and many other fascinating exhibits.

Apple Pie

"I've used this recipe for 34 years! My family loves it."

Barbara Newland—Newland's Resort, Lakeview

1 (9-inch) unbaked PIE SHELL
3-4 GRANNY SMITH APPLES, peeled, cored and thinly sliced
1/2 cup SUGAR
1 tsp. CINNAMON
1/3 cup MARGARINE
1/2 cup SUGAR
3/4 cup FLOUR
1/3 cup LIGHT CORN SYRUP

Preheat oven to 400°. Generously fill pie shell with apple slices. Mix sugar and cinnamon together; sprinkle over the apples. In a bowl, combine margarine, sugar and flour; sprinkle over the apple slices. Drizzle corn syrup in small circles on top. Place pie on bottom oven rack and bake for 25 minutes. Move pie to center oven rack and bake for 25 minutes longer.

Brown Sugar Marshmallow Fudge

"This is my own recipe that I have used since 1976. I have given it to many friends and family members."

Fern Dutiel—Wheelersburg

1 box (16 oz.) BROWN SUGAR
6 oz. EVAPORATED MILK
1/2 stick MARGARINE
Dash of SALT

1 tsp. VANILLA
3 1/2 oz. MARSHMALLOW
    CREAM
1/2 cup PEANUT BUTTER

In a saucepan, combine brown sugar and milk. Cook over medium heat until mixture thickens; remove from heat. Stir in margarine and beat well. Add salt, vanilla, marshmallow cream and peanut butter. Beat until mixture cools slightly. Pour into baking pan and allow to cool completely before dividing into squares.

Pineapple Cake with Cream Cheese Frosting

"This is a very easy cake to make and a family favorite!"

Bessie L. Spencer—Greenville

2 cups FLOUR
2 cups SUGAR
2 EGGS, beaten

2 tsp. BAKING SODA
1 can (20 oz.) CRUSHED
  PINEAPPLE, with juice

Preheat oven to 350°. In a mixing bowl, combine all ingredients and mix well. Pour into a 13 x 9 pan. Bake for 30 minutes or until center springs back after a light touch. Allow cake to cool slightly, but while still warm, spread with *Cream Cheese Frosting.*

Cream Cheese Frosting

1 pkg. (8 oz.) CREAM CHEESE,
  softened
1 stick BUTTER, softened

1 cup POWDERED SUGAR
1 tsp. VANILLA
1 tsp. MILK

In a bowl, combine all ingredients and blend well.

Shaker Pie

"The Shakers had a very large community in this area from the 1800s to the 1900s. They left behind the art of simplicity in crafting furniture and in cooking. This pie is a perfect example."

Joan McCarren—Cedar Hill B & B in the Woods, Wilmington

1/3 cup FLOUR
1 cup packed BROWN SUGAR
1 (9-inch) unbaked PIE SHELL
2 cups LIGHT CREAM

1 tsp. VANILLA
1 stick BUTTER
1 tsp. NUTMEG

In a bowl, thoroughly mix flour and brown sugar together; spread evenly in bottom of pie shell. Combine cream and vanilla and pour into pie shell. Slice butter into 12-16 pieces and distribute evenly over top; sprinkle with nutmeg. Bake at 350° for 40-45 minutes or until firm.

Grandma's Blue Ribbon Angel Food Cake

"My grandmother was famous for this recipe. It always took top honors at the county fair. It is so soft, she preferred to cut it with a thread!"

Jonna Cronebaugh—Olde World B & B, Dover

1 1/4 cups SWANS DOWN® CAKE FLOUR	1/4 tsp. SALT
	1 1/4 tsp. CREAM OF TARTAR
2 cups SUGAR	1 tsp. VANILLA
1 1/2 cups EGG WHITES	

Sift flour. Add 1/2 cup sugar and sift mixture 4 times. Combine egg whites, salt, cream of tartar and vanilla and beat until egg whites stand in soft peaks. Add remaining sugar in 3 additions, beating 25 times after each addition. Fold in sugar/ flour mixture in 4 additions and fold over 15 times after each addition. Pour into an ungreased angel food cake pan; run a knife around the outside to release air pockets. Bake at 375° for 35-40 minutes.

Spicebush Berry Cookies

"We think this makes an excellent holiday cookie!"

Chris Chmiel—Integration Acres, Albany

1 1/2 cups WHOLE-WHEAT FLOUR	1 EGG, lightly beaten
	2 tsp. dried ground
1 1/2 tsp. BAKING POWDER	SPICEBUSH BERRIES
1/2 tsp. SALT	1 ts. VANILLA
3 Tbsp. BUTTER, softened	3 Tbsp. WATER
1/2 cup packed BROWN SUGAR	POWDERED SUGAR

Sift flour, baking powder and salt together. Cream butter with sugar; beat in egg, berries, vanilla and water. Gradually add creamed mixture to flour mixture, mixing well after each addition. Divide dough in half and roll each into 1 1/2" diameter logs. Wrap in waxed paper and refrigerate for 2 hours. Preheat oven to 375°. Cut logs into 1/4" thick slices and place on a cookie sheet. Bake 10-12 minutes. While still warm, coat with powdered sugar.

Buckeye Chocolate Peanut Butter Cake

"My husband calls this my 'signature cake' because everyone requests it for special occasions. It's easy to make and delicious!"

Diane Dirksen—Cridersville

1 box (18.25 oz.) YELLOW CAKE MIX
1/2 cup CREAMY PEANUT BUTTER

Prepare cake mix according to package directions. Stir in peanut butter. Pour batter into 2 greased and floured 9-inch cake pans. Bake at 350° for 25 minutes; allow to cool completely. Spread *Chocolate Peanut Butter Frosting* between layers of the cake, then evenly on the top and sides.

Chocolate Peanut Butter Frosting

3/4 cup HERSHEY'S® CHOCOLATE SYRUP
1 pkg. (6 oz.) SEMI-SWEET CHOCOLATE CHIPS
2 cups CREAMY PEANUT BUTTER
1 cup POWDERED SUGAR
1/4 cup MILK

In a small, heavy saucepan, combine chocolate syrup and chocolate chips. Heat over low heat, stirring constantly, until chocolate is melted and mixture is smooth. Transfer to a large bowl and beat in peanut butter, then powdered sugar and then milk; beat until smooth.

Akron

Founded in 1825, Akron (from the Greek word "akros", meaning "high point") was once the world's largest manufacturer of tires. Today, some of those same Akron manufacturers have turned to scientific research projects including the design and fitting of the original space suits worn by U.S. astronauts. Each August, the All-American Soap Box Derby and the World Series of Golf attract visitors from all over the world.

Fruit Pizza

"This recipe is from the kitchen of a friend, Dorothy Meyer. Abell Berry Farm encourages families to spend time gathering fresh fruit, relaxing in the 'barn room' (antiques from the family) and picnicking on the grounds around the fishing pond."

Sam & Jeanette Abell—Abell Berry Farm, Kent

Glaze:
1/2 cup SUGAR
1/2 cup ORANGE JUICE
1/4 cup WATER
2 Tbsp. LEMON JUICE
1 1/2 Tbsp. CORNSTARCH

1 pkg. (20 oz.) SUGAR COOKIE MIX

Pizza Topping:
1 pkg. (8 oz.) CREAM
    CHEESE, softened
4 oz. COOL WHIP®
Sliced PEACHES
BLUEBERRIES

Sliced BANANAS
Sliced CANTALOUPE
Sliced KIWI, halved
MARASCHINO CHERRIES

    Combine glaze ingredients in a saucepan and bring to a boil, stirring often; allow to cool. Prepare cookie mix according to package directions. Spread dough on a greased pizza pan. Bake at 375° for 5 minutes; allow to cool. In a bowl, beat cream cheese until smooth; fold in Cool Whip. Spread mixture over cooled crust. Arrange sliced fruit and berries on top, in alternating circles, from the outside toward the center ending with a circle of kiwi in the middle. Pile cherries in center. Spoon glaze over fruit, covering completely. Refrigerate until ready to serve.

Historic Glassworks

The Abell Berry Farm is located on the site of the historic Franklin Glass Company, famous for its green / blue glassworks in the 1800s. Kilns from the glassworks have been excavated by Kent Sate University and are on display at Hale Homestead, Summit County.

Snickerdoodles

These still-popular cookies date as far back as the Civil War. At that time they often included dried currants or raisins. There is no baking powder in these cookies (it was not readily available in the 1860s). The cream of tartar and saleratus (baking soda) were used as a substitute. The cookies will puff up, then flatten out and have crinkled tops.

1 cup BUTTER, softened	2 3/4 cups FLOUR
1 1/2 teacupfuls SUGAR	2 tsp. CREAM OF TARTAR
2 EGGS	1 tsp. SALERATUS (baking
12 tsp. SALT	soda)

Cream butter, gradually adding sugar and then eggs. Sift dry ingredients together; and then gradually beat into creamed mixture. Chill. Form dough into balls the size of small walnuts. Roll in a mixture of **2 Tbsp. SUGAR** and **2 tsp. CINNAMON.** Place rolls on an ungreased cookie sheet and bake at 400° until lightly browned but still soft (about 10 minutes).

Makes 60 cookies.

Best Ever Brownies

"While my husband was in college, he used to make daily visits to a nearby bakery. He loved these brownies so much that the owner finally gave him his recipe."

Judy Zakutny—Elyria

4 oz. UNSWEETENED CHOCOLATE	1 1/4 cups FLOUR
2/3 cup SHORTENING	1 tsp. SALT
2 cups SUGAR	1 tsp. BAKING POWDER
4 EGGS	1 cup chopped NUTS
1 tsp. VANILLA	FROSTING (optional)

Melt chocolate and shortening in a saucepan. Mix sugar, eggs and vanilla into chocolate mixture. Stir in all remaining ingredients. Pour batter into a well-greased and floured 13 x 9 baking pan. Bake in a preheated 350° oven for 30 minutes or until brownies pull away from sides of pan. Let cool completely before frosting, if desired.

★ ★ ★ ★ *Cooking Across America* ★ ★ ★ ★

Ohio Food Festival Sampler

April/May

Geauga County Maple Festival, Chardon
Dandelion May Fest, Dover
Springtime in Ohio, Findlay
May Herb & Craft Festival, Gahanna
Miamisburg Spring Fling, Miamisburg
Moonshine Festival, New Straitsville
Norwalk Jaycees Strawberry Fest., Norwalk
Port Clinton Walleye Festival, Port Clinton
Utica Old Fashion Ice Cream Festival, Utica

June/July

Troy Strawberry Festival, Troy
Banana Split Festival, Wilmington
Festival of the Fish, Vermilion
Strawberry Festival, Jefferson
London Strawberry Festival, London
Festival Latino, Columbus

August

Ohio State Fair, Columbus
Bucyrus Bratwurst Festival, Bucyrus
Farmers Harvest Days, Farmersville
N. Ridgeville Corn Festival, N. Ridgeville
Sweet Corn Festival, Fairborn
Slavic Village Harvest Festival, Cleveland
Milan Melon Festival, Milan
Tuscarawas County Italian-American
    Festival, New Philadelphia
W. Jefferson Annual Ox Roast, W.Jefferson

September

American Soya Festival, Amanda
Barnesville Pumpkin Festival, Barnesville
Circleville Pumpkin Show, Circleville
Ole Market Day, Milan
Fredericktown Tomato Show, Fredericktown
Geneva Area Grape Jamboree, Geneva
Waynesburg Heritage Days, Waynesburg
Octoberfest, Vandalia
Milan Melon Festival, Milan
Reynoldsburg Tomato Festival, Reynoldsburg
Marion Popcorn Festival, Marion

Mantua Potato Festival, Mantua
Village Peddler Festival, Jefferson
Yankee Peddler Festival, Canal Fulton
Xenia Old Fashioned Days Festival, Xenia
Jackson County Apple Festival, Jackson
Johnny Appleseed Festival, Brunswick
Oak Harbor Apple Festival, Oak Harbor
Ohio Gourd Show, Mt. Gilead
Ohio Swiss Festival, Sugarcreek
Oldtime Farming Festival, Centerburg
Pawpaw Festival, Albany
Woosterfest, Wooster
Bremen Oktoberfest, Bremen
Applefest, Lebanon
Aullwood Apple Fest, Dayton
Loyal Oak Cider Fest, Norton
Harvest Festival, Cincinnati
Soakum Festival, Caldwell
Sweet Corn Festival, Inc., Millersport
Tiffin-Seneca Heritage Festival, Tiffin

October

Wonderful World of Ohio Mart, Akron
Beaver Oktoberfest, Beaver
Oktoberfest, Cuyahoga Falls
Minster Oktoberfest, Minster
Sorghum Makin', Pond Creek
Apple Dumpling Festival, Shreve
Zoar Applefest, Zoar
Champaign County Oktoberfest, Urbana
Octoberfest, Zanesville
Bob Evans Farm Festival, Rio Grande
Ohio Sauerkraut Festival, Waynesville
Olde Thyme Herb Fair, Manchester
The Circleville Pumpkin Show, Circleville
Van Wert County Apple Festival, Van Wert
Apple Butter Stirrin', Coshocton
Harvest Festival, Stow

November

Columbus International Festival, Columbus
Country Store, Obetz

 88 *Ohio Food Festival Sampler*

Index

★ ★ ★ ★ *Cooking Across America* ★ ★ ★ ★

Index (Continued)

Index (Continued)

★ ★ ★ ★ *Cooking Across America* ★ ★ ★ ★

Index (Continued)

Ohio Cook Book Contributors

Ohio Cook Book Contributors 93

More cookbooks from Golden West Publishers

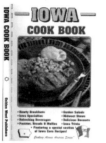

IOWA COOK BOOK

Recipes from across America's heartland. From *Indian Two-Corn Pudding* to *Pork Chops Braised in White Wine* this cookbook presents home-grown favorites and encompasses both ethnic traditions and gourmet specialties. A special section entitled "Iowa Corn Recipes" highlights this state's most famous export.

5 1/2 x 8 1/2 — 96 pages . . . $6.95

ILLINOIS COOK BOOK

Enjoy the flavors of Illinois! Over 100 recipes that celebrate Illinois. *Reuben in the Round, Pork Medallions in Herb Sauce, Autumn's Swiss Supper, Carrot Soufflé, Sky High Honey Biscuits* and *Rhubarb Cream Pie,* to name just a few. Includes fascinating facts and trivia.

5 1/2 x 8 1/2 — 96 pages . . . $6.95

KANSAS COOK BOOK

Over 125 luscious recipes capture the rich cultural and historical charm of Kansas. Traditional and contemporary recipes include favorites such as *Pumpkin Dumplin's with Apple Chutney, Sunflower Salad, Kansas Beef Strogonoff, Corn Fritters* and *Yellow Brick Road Cake.* Entertaining Kansas trivia and facts.

5 1/2 x 8 1/2 — 96 pages . . . $6.95

MINNESOTA COOK BOOK

Featuring Minnesota's rich blend of cultures and culinary traditions. Eye-opening breakfast and brunch selections, distinctive soup and salad recipes, savory main and side dishes and delicious desserts. From *Zucchini Pancakes* to *Swedish Almond Rusks,* you'll find recipes for every occasion!

5 1/2 x 8 1/2 — 96 pages . . . $6.95

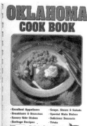

OKLAHOMA COOK BOOK

From *Indian Fry Bread* to *Chicken Fried Steak* and from *Pineapple-Zucchini Bread* to *Shoo-fly Pie,* this cookbook presents homegrown recipes that encompass the many ethnic traditions that are part of this state's history. Enjoy these unique down-home tastes of Oklahoma cooking!

5 1/2 x 8 1/2 — 96 pages . . . $6.95

More cookbooks from Golden West Publishers

APPLE LOVERS COOK BOOK

Celebrating America's favorite—the apple! 150 recipes for main and side dishes, appetizers, salads, breads, muffins, cakes, pies, desserts, beverages and preserves; all kitchen-tested!

5 1/2 x 8 1/2 — 120 Pages . . . $6.95

BERRY LOVERS COOK BOOK

Berrylicious recipes for enjoying these natural wonders. From *Blueberry Muffins, Strawberry Cheesecake* and *Raspberry Sticky Rolls* to *Boysenberry Mint Frosty* or *Gooseberry Crunch,* you will find tasty recipes that will bring raves from your friends and family. Includes berry facts and trivia.

5 1/2 x 8 1/2 — 96 Pages . . . $6.95

CORN LOVERS COOK BOOK

Over 100 delicious recipes featuring America's favorite! Try *Corn Chowder, Corn Soufflé, Apple Cornbread* or *Caramel Corn,* to name a few. You will find a tempting recipe for every occasion in this collection. Includes corn facts and trivia, too!

5 1/2 x 8 1/2 — 88 pages . . . $6.95

THE JOY OF MUFFINS

The International Muffin Cook Book

Recipes for *German Streusel, Finnish Cranberry, Italian Amaretto, Greek Baklava, Chinese Almond, Jamaican Banana, Swiss Fondue,* microwave section and ten recipes for oat bran muffins . . . 150 recipes in all!

5 1/2 x 8 1/2 — 120 Pages . . . $6.95

VEGGIE LOVERS COOK BOOK

Everyone will love these no-cholesterol, no-animal recipes! Over 200 nutritious, flavorful recipes by Chef Morty Star. Includes a foreword by Dr. Michael Klaper. Nutritional analysis for each recipe to help you plan a healthy diet.

5 1/2 x 8 1/2 — 128 pages . . . $6.95

ORDER BLANK

GOLDEN WEST PUBLISHERS

☼ 4113 N. Longview Ave. • Phoenix, AZ 85014

www.goldenwestpublishers.com • **1-800-658-5830** • FAX 602-279-6901

Qty	Title	Price	Amount
	Apple Lovers Cook Book	6.95	
	Bean Lovers Cook Book	6.95	
	Berry Lovers Cook Book	6.95	
	Best Barbecue Recipes	6.95	
	Chili-Lovers' Cook Book	6.95	
	Corn Lovers Cook Book	6.95	
	Easy Recipes for Wild Game & Fish	6.95	
	Illinois Cook Book	6.95	
	Indiana Cook Book	6.95	
	Iowa Cook Book	6.95	
	Joy of Muffins	6.95	
	Kansas Cook Book	6.95	
	Minnesota Cook Book	6.95	
	Missouri Cook Book	6.95	
	Ohio Cook Book	6.95	
	Oklahoma Cook Book	6.95	
	Pumpkin Lovers Cook Book	6.95	
	Salsa Lovers Cook Book	6.95	
	Veggie Lovers Cook Book	6.95	
	Wisconsin Cook Book	6.95	
Shipping & Handling Add:	United States $3.00 Canada & Mexico $5.00—All others $12.00		

☐ My Check or Money Order Enclosed

☐ MasterCard ☐ VISA ($20 credit card minimum)

Total $ _____

(Payable in U.S. funds)

Acct. No. _____ Exp. Date _____

Signature _____

Name _____ Phone _____

Address _____

City/State/Zip _____

Call for a FREE catalog of all of our titles

This order blank may be photo copied.

2/02

Ohio Ck Bk